200 Nouns 2,000 Sentences
Latin American Spanish
Frequency List

200 Nouns 2,000 Sentences
Latin American Spanish
Frequency List

ISBN: 978-1-952161-15-5

www.L2Press.com

First Edition

This Spanish book series is dedicated to

Alexander Argüelles, Luca Lampariello, and Mikel Telleria Mujika

for their practical contributions to self-taught language learners.

Thank you.

Introduction

This book introduces the 200 most frequent Spanish nouns, which account for over half of the nouns you'll encounter in everyday conversation and writing. Each noun is presented through 10 simple example sentences that highlight its most common meaning, as well as gender and number forms. But you're not just learning nouns in isolation. Each noun appears alongside the words it frequently pairs with, including common adjectives, verbs, adverbs, and prepositions that native speakers use all the time. As a result, you'll repeatedly see and absorb the vocabulary that most often appears with these high-frequency nouns. Over the course of the book, this adds up to exposure to thousands of useful words and patterns. Think of this book not just as a guide to 200 nouns, but as a gateway to the core vocabulary and patterns that shape natural, everyday Spanish.

The beauty of this method lies in its simplicity. Short, easy-to-understand sentences allow you to focus on building a solid foundation without feeling overwhelmed. Experienced language learners tend to make faster progress when they're exposed to large amounts of clear, understandable language rather than focusing heavily on grammar rules. With that in mind, you'll learn primarily through meaningful repetition and practical examples while developing the ability to infer meaning from context, one of the most valuable skills for long-term proficiency and fluency. By encountering words and structures repeatedly in various meaningful contexts, you'll gradually develop an intuitive feel for Spanish that goes beyond memorization.

By the time you complete this book and its companions, "200 Verbs" and "200 Adjectives", you'll have built a vocabulary and intuition strong enough to dive into authentic content made for native Spanish speakers. While this book introduces many common nouns and adjectives in context, the companion books give them the dedicated, systematic treatment they deserve, ensuring the highest-frequency words in each category are fully covered, not just encountered in passing. Together, these three books cover the highest-frequency words across the most essential categories of Spanish, giving you a solid, well-rounded foundation.

The Spanish in this book reflects Latin American usage, with a slight emphasis on Mexico. The audio is read by a native Mexican speaker, so you'll hear a clear, neutral Mexican accent throughout. The vocabulary is easily understood across Latin America (and even Spain), while staying grounded in everyday Mexican usage. Mexico is home to more Spanish speakers than any other country, making its variety of Spanish an ideal foundation for anyone learning the language.

Audio is where everything comes together. Reading helps you recognize patterns, but listening and speaking is what turns those patterns into real, usable language. When you hear the sentences spoken clearly and naturally, you begin to internalize pronunciation, rhythm, and flow. Your Spanish will start to feel more automatic and authentic. The complete audio for this book allows you to reinforce every sentence through repeated exposure, helping you connect what you see on the page with how it actually sounds. You can listen while reading, repeat aloud while reading, or listen on its own to train your ear. This kind of consistent repetition is the fastest way to build real fluency. If you want to move beyond recognizing Spanish to truly understanding and using it, combining the book with the audio is essential. The full audio of this book is available for purchase at L2Press.com.

Ready to start your Spanish journey the smart and efficient way? This book offers you a clear path to success. Whether your goal is to connect with Spanish-speaking friends, enhance your career opportunities, or immerse yourself in the rich culture of Mexico, Colombia, and other Spanish-speaking countries, this book will get you there faster and more effectively than traditional grammar-based approaches. Don't waste time on inefficient learning methods. Begin your transformation into a confident Spanish speaker today with this focused and practical approach to language learning.

How to use this book

Build Spanish fluency by rotating through three powerful techniques: shadowing, reading aloud, active recall:

- Shadowing is a form of active listening. Listen to the audio and repeat it aloud nearly simultaneously, following the speaker like a shadow. You can do this while reading the Spanish, the English, or without looking at the text. Focus on sounding like the native speaker. Pay attention to vowel sounds, vowel length, new consonant sounds, stress, and intonation.
- Reading aloud bridges the gap between written and spoken Spanish. Simply read the sentences out loud at your own pace. This helps you build confidence, improve pronunciation, and get used to hearing your own voice in Spanish.
- Active recall here means translating from English into Spanish. Cover the Spanish and try to produce the Spanish you've been practicing. It's the most effective and challenging step, as it forces your brain to retrieve the language instead of just recognizing it.

Note that you speak aloud in each step. This is critical for training your mouth and tongue. Language is a physical skill as much as a mental one, and your ability to understand and recall Spanish will only take you so far if your mouth isn't trained to produce it. Whether you are shadowing, reading aloud, or doing active recall, speaking in every step builds the muscle memory needed to form sounds quickly, smoothly, and naturally. This repeated, active production is what turns passive knowledge into real speaking ability.

These three techniques work together as a single learning loop that you repeat with the same material. Rather than moving on to new material each day, you return to the same sentences in different ways. You begin by hearing and imitating the language through shadowing, which builds familiarity with the sounds and rhythm. Then you reinforce that familiarity by reading aloud at your own pace, giving your brain more time to process and your mouth more time to practice. Finally, you test and strengthen what you've learned through active recall, forcing yourself to produce the language on your own. Each step prepares you for the next, and each pass through the loop deepens your understanding and ability. Over time, what once felt unfamiliar will become more automatic.

I recommend spending about 30 minutes per day with this book. On the first day, shadow six pages. On the second day, go back to those same six pages and read them aloud at your own pace. On the third day, cover the Spanish and try to actively recall the sentences by translating from English. If you can produce at least half of them with reasonable accuracy, that's a good sign you're ready to move on to the next set of pages. If not, simply repeat the cycle. There's no need to rush. Going back over the same material is not a setback. It's how you learn. Some sections will click quickly, while others may take an extra pass or two. The goal is steady progress and growing familiarity, not perfection.

Your goal is not to memorize every sentence in this book. Your goal is exposure. By working through many examples of the most common verbs and structures, you start to recognize patterns without having to think about them. You'll encounter the same words and constructions multiple times in slightly different contexts, and your brain will absorb them naturally over time. Some sentences will stick and others won't, and that's perfectly fine. What matters is building a deep familiarity with how Spanish works. That familiarity is what allows you to understand real Spanish and respond with confidence.

Recommended routine

A 3-day loop that will produce excellent results (Day 1 - Shadow, Day 2 - Read aloud, Day 3 - Active recall):

Day 1 of pages 1-6	Shadow Spanish twice (first while looking at Spanish & then while looking at English)
Day 2 of pages 1-6	Read Spanish aloud, look at English translation, read Spanish aloud again
Day 3 of pages 1-6	Active recall (cover the Spanish and translate the English into Spanish aloud)
Day 1 of pages 7-12	Shadow Spanish twice (first while looking at Spanish & then while looking at English)
Day 2 of pages 7-12	Read Spanish aloud, look at English translation, read Spanish aloud again
Day 3 of pages 7-12	Active recall (cover the Spanish and translate the English into Spanish aloud)
Day 1 of pages 13-18	Shadow Spanish twice (first while looking at Spanish & then while looking at English)
Day 2 of pages 13-18	Read Spanish aloud, look at English translation, read Spanish aloud again
Day 3 of pages 13-18	Active recall (cover the Spanish and translate the English into Spanish aloud)
Day 1 of pages 19-24	Shadow Spanish twice (first while looking at Spanish & then while looking at English)
Day 2 of pages 19-24	Read Spanish aloud, look at English translation, read Spanish aloud again
Day 3 of pages 19-24	Active recall (cover the Spanish and translate the English into Spanish aloud)
Day 1 of pages 25-30	Shadow Spanish twice (first while looking at Spanish & then while looking at English)
Day 2 of pages 25-30	Read Spanish aloud, look at English translation, read Spanish aloud again
Day 3 of pages 25-30	Active recall (cover the Spanish and translate the English into Spanish aloud)
Day 1 of pages 31-36	Shadow Spanish twice (first while looking at Spanish & then while looking at English)
Day 2 of pages 31-36	Read Spanish aloud, look at English translation, read Spanish aloud again
Day 3 of pages 31-36	Active recall (cover the Spanish and translate the English into Spanish aloud)
Day 1 of pages 37-42	Shadow Spanish twice (first while looking at Spanish & then while looking at English)
Day 2 of pages 37-42	Read Spanish aloud, look at English translation, read Spanish aloud again
Day 3 of pages 37-42	Active recall (cover the Spanish and translate the English into Spanish aloud)
Day 1 of pages 43-48	Shadow Spanish twice (first while looking at Spanish & then while looking at English)
Day 2 of pages 43-48	Read Spanish aloud, look at English translation, read Spanish aloud again
Day 3 of pages 43-48	Active recall (cover the Spanish and translate the English into Spanish aloud)
Day 1 of pages 49-54	Shadow Spanish twice (first while looking at Spanish & then while looking at English)
Day 2 of pages 49-54	Read Spanish aloud, look at English translation, read Spanish aloud again
Day 3 of pages 49-54	Active recall (cover the Spanish and translate the English into Spanish aloud)
Day 1 of pages 55-60	Shadow Spanish twice (first while looking at Spanish & then while looking at English)
Day 2 of pages 55-60	Read Spanish aloud, look at English translation, read Spanish aloud again
Day 3 of pages 55-60	Active recall (cover the Spanish and translate the English into Spanish aloud)
Day 1 of pages 61-67	Shadow Spanish twice (first while looking at Spanish & then while looking at English)
Day 2 of pages 61-67	Read Spanish aloud, look at English translation, read Spanish aloud again
Day 3 of pages 61-67	Active recall (cover the Spanish and translate the English into Spanish aloud)

What to do after this book series

This book series gives you a strong, intermediate-level foundation in Spanish. Once you finish it, the next step is to move into real-world Spanish, where your progress will come from continued exposure, active use, and consistent practice. Here are some of the most effective ways to keep improving with native materials.

Reading: There are two main methods language learners use to read, intensive reading and extensive reading. Intensive reading means working through a small amount of text carefully, looking up words and paying attention to grammar and sentence structure. Extensive reading means reading quickly and fluidly for enjoyment, without stopping to look things up, to build overall exposure to the language. Do both. Read books written for native speakers, starting with simpler ones, and consider reading Spanish versions of books you've already read and know well. Choose topics and genres you enjoy. Over time, extensive reading builds familiarity with vocabulary and structure, while intensive reading helps you understand the details more deeply. Don't forget to read aloud some of the time.

Watching and Listening: Watch TV shows, movies, and listen to podcasts in Spanish on topics you already enjoy. In the beginning, look for simpler native content. Then gradually move on to more advanced content, even if you don't catch everything. To get the most out of any episode, read a transcript beforehand to prime your brain and familiarize yourself with new words and phrases. Then watch or listen attentively and review the transcript afterward. Repeat this process as often as you like, while also exposing yourself to a wide variety of content. Over time, your ear will adapt, your vocabulary will grow, and what once felt confusing will start to feel natural.

Speaking: Find a native speaker and converse with them on a consistent basis. The ideal practice partner is patient and will not simply correct your errors but will prompt you to self-correct and express your ideas more clearly. If you want to speak fluently, there is no substitute for regular conversation. Try to schedule consistent sessions, even if they are short, and focus on communicating your thoughts rather than speaking perfectly. Mistakes are part of the process. Prepare a few topics or questions beforehand to keep the conversation flowing, and reuse phrases you've learned so they become automatic. You will eventually notice that what once required effort starts to come naturally, and your confidence will grow with each interaction.

Language Islands: A language island is a personal collection of sentences built around specific situations in your own life, practiced until they become automatic so the language is already there when you need it. The idea is to build small islands of fluency around moments you're likely to find yourself in, such as introducing yourself, ordering food, talking about your work or your family. To create one, write about 20 simple, natural sentences you would actually say in that situation, then practice them out loud until they feel effortless. Eventually you can expand their complexity by adding details, changing verb tenses, and swapping vocabulary. Over time, your islands grow and connect, and your speech becomes faster, more natural, and more confident.

Travel and Immersion: Visit a Spanish-speaking country and avoid using any language but Spanish. When you're immersed, every interaction becomes a lesson. The pressure of real communication accelerates your progress in a way that structured study simply cannot. You will make mistakes and occasionally feel lost, but that discomfort is exactly what helps the language to click. Even short trips can lead to noticeable progress if you fully commit to using Spanish.

1 – cosa

thing

¿Qué es esta cosa?
What is this thing?

Siempre pasa la misma cosa.
The same thing always happens.

Una cosa llevó a la otra.
One thing led to another.

No es gran cosa.
It's no big deal.

Una cosa es hablar y otra hacer.
It's one thing to talk and another to do.

Tengo muchas cosas que hacer.
I have many things to do.

Las cosas ya no son como solían ser.
Things aren't like they used to be.

Las cosas cambian.
Things change.

No prometas cosas que no cumplirás.
Don't promise things you won't do.

Están pasando cosas raras.
Strange things are happening.

2 – tiempo

time, weather

No tengo tiempo para ir al cine hoy.
I don't have time to go to the movies today.

No hay tiempo que perder.
There's no time to lose.

Me gusta pasar tiempo con mi familia.
I like spending time with my family.

Valora el tiempo que tienes con ellos.
Value the time you have with them.

¿Cómo está el tiempo?
How's the weather?

Hace buen tiempo hoy.
The weather is nice today.

¿Cómo va a estar el tiempo mañana?
How's the weather going to be tomorrow?

¿Cómo estuvo el tiempo en tu viaje?
How was the weather on your trip?

Estos son tiempos difíciles para todos.
These are difficult times for everyone.

Los tiempos modernos traen nuevos desafíos.
Modern times bring new challenges.

3 – año

year

¡Feliz Año Nuevo!
Happy New Year!

Este año ha pasado volando.
This year has flown by.

A finales de año siempre hay muchas fiestas.
At the end of the year, there are always many parties.

Este fue el mejor año de mi vida.
This was the best year of my life.

Este año quiero viajar más.
This year I want to travel more.

He estado viviendo aquí por un año.
I've been living here for a year.

No lo he visto en años.
I haven't seen him in years.

Mis abuelos estuvieron casados cincuenta años.
My grandparents were married for fifty years.

Ella cumplió quince años hace poco.
She recently turned fifteen.

En los años ochenta la música era diferente.
In the eighties the music was different.

4 – día

Que tengas un buen día.
El día está perfecto para salir.
Hoy es un día perfecto para ir a la playa.
Qué día tan loco, no paré un segundo.
Algún día voy a viajar por todo el mundo.
Los últimos días han estado tranquilos.
Cada día cuenta, pero algunos días marcan tu vida.
Caminamos diez días por los Alpes franceses.
Esos fueron los mejores días de mi vida.
Llevo días pensando en eso.

day

Have a good day.
The day is perfect for going out.
Today is a perfect day to go to the beach.
What a crazy day, I didn't stop for a second.
Someday I'm going to travel around the world.
The last few days have been calm.
Every day counts, but some days mark your life.
We hiked for ten days through the French Alps.
Those were the best days of my life.
I've been thinking about that for days.

5 – persona

Esa persona ya no trabaja aquí.
Conocí a una persona interesante en la fiesta.
Nunca antes había visto a esa persona.
No soy el tipo de persona que se rinde fácilmente.
Necesitamos contratar a una persona con experiencia.
En el concierto había como diez mil personas.
¿Cuántas personas van a venir a la cena?
Varias personas me preguntaron por lo mismo.
Las personas cambian con el tiempo.
Muchas personas no saben eso.

person

That person doesn't work here anymore.
I met an interesting person at the party.
I had never seen that person before.
I'm not the type of person who gives up easily.
We need to hire a person with experience.
At the concert there were like ten thousand people.
How many people are coming to dinner?
Several people asked me about the same thing.
People change over time.
Many people don't know that.

6 – vida

La vida es corta, disfrútala.
Mi vida cambió después de ese viaje.
La vida se va volando, así que aprovéchala.
Esa decisión marcó mi vida.
A veces la vida no es justa.
La vida de mi abuela fue larga y feliz.
La vida en el campo es más tranquila.
Nuestras vidas son muy distintas.
Mis hijos tienen vidas muy ocupadas.
Las vacunas han salvado millones de vidas.

life

Life is short, enjoy it.
My life changed after that trip.
Life flies by, so make the most of it.
That decision marked my life.
Sometimes life isn't fair.
My grandmother's life was long and happy.
Life in the countryside is calmer.
Our lives are very different.
My kids have very busy lives.
Vaccines have saved millions of lives.

7 – casa	**house**
No hay nadie en casa ahora.	There's nobody home right now.
Me siento en casa aquí.	I feel at home here.
¿Vas a estar en casa en la tarde?	Are you going to be home in the afternoon?
Voy a estar en casa todo el día.	I'm going to be home all day.
¿Ya llegaste a casa?	Did you get home already?
Trabajo desde casa los viernes.	I work from home on Fridays.
Las casas de Guanajuato son de colores.	The houses in Guanajuato are colorful.
Las casas en este barrio son muy caras.	The houses in this neighborhood are very expensive.
Las casas de esta calle son bonitas.	The houses on this street are pretty.
Aquí las casas se venden rápido.	Here the houses sell quickly.

8 – vez	**time, occasion, instance**
¿Cuándo fue la última vez que nos vimos?	When was the last time we saw each other?
Dime una vez más qué tengo que hacer.	Tell me one more time what I need to do.
Es la primera vez que he visto algo así.	It's the first time I've seen something like that.
Cada vez que paso por ahí, me acuerdo de ti.	Every time I pass by there, I remember you.
Voy al gimnasio una vez por semana.	I go to the gym once a week.
Hay veces que prefiero estar solo.	There are times when I prefer to be alone.
He ido pocas veces al cine este año.	I've gone to the movies only a few times this year.
Muchas veces pienso en cambiar de trabajo.	Many times I think about changing jobs.
Algunas veces todo sale como uno quiere.	Sometimes everything turns out the way one wants.
A veces me cuesta dormir.	Sometimes I have trouble sleeping.

9 – forma	**shape, way, form**
Necesito ponerme en forma.	I need to get in shape.
Estoy en muy buena forma este año.	I'm in very good shape this year.
Esa nube tiene forma de gato.	That cloud is shaped like a cat.
La forma del corazón es simbólica.	The shape of the heart is symbolic.
No hay forma de entrar sin clave.	There's no way to enter without a code.
Buscamos una forma de resolver el problema.	We're looking for a way to solve the problem.
La forma en que lo explicó fue muy clara.	The way he explained it was very clear.
Hice un pastel en forma de corazón para mi esposa.	I made a heart-shaped cake for my wife.
Las formas de vida marina son fascinantes.	Marine life forms are fascinating.
Las formas geométricas son importantes en arte.	Geometric shapes are important in art.

10 – parte

part

¿De qué parte de México eres? — What part of Mexico are you from?
Me encantó esa parte del libro. — I loved that part of the book.
La mejor parte de la película fue el final. — The best part of the movie was the ending.
No entiendo esta parte de la tarea. — I don't understand this part of the homework.
En gran parte tienes razón. — You're right for the most part.
¿Qué parte no entendiste? — Which part didn't you understand?
No entiendo algunas partes. — I don't understand some parts.
Todas las partes encajan perfectamente. — All the parts fit perfectly.
Ya revisé todas las partes. — I already checked all the parts.
Faltan varias partes. — Several parts are missing.

11 – mundo

world

Mi familia es mi mundo. — My family is my world.
Hay mucha gente en el mundo. — There are many people in the world.
Este libro me cambió la forma de ver el mundo. — This book changed the way I see the world.
Todo el mundo viene a la fiesta. — Everyone is coming to the party.
No haría eso por nada del mundo. — I wouldn't do that for anything in the world.
No es el fin del mundo. — It's not the end of the world.
En un mundo ideal, todo sería diferente. — In an ideal world, everything would be different.
Esos dos vienen de mundos diferentes. — Those two come from different worlds.
Sus mundos se juntaron cuando se casaron. — Their worlds came together when they got married.
Vivimos en mundos diferentes. — We live in different worlds.

12 – gente

people

La gente entra y sale de tu vida. — People come and go from your life.
La gente ya no confía en los políticos. — People no longer trust politicians.
La gente buena todavía existe. — Good people still exist.
Me gusta observar a la gente en el parque. — I like watching people in the park.
La gente de esa zona habla muy rápido. — People from that area speak very fast.
Conocí gente interesante en la fiesta. — I met interesting people at the party.
No toda la gente piensa igual. — Not all people think the same.
La gente joven usa mucho las redes sociales. — Young people use social media a lot.
La gente mayor merece nuestro respeto. — Elderly people deserve our respect.
Ella es buena gente. — She's good people.

13 – trabajo | **work, job**

Voy al trabajo. | I'm going to work.
Salgo del trabajo a las cinco. | I get off work at five.
Me ofrecieron un trabajo mejor pagado. | They offered me a better-paid job.
¿Cómo te fue hoy en el trabajo? | How did it go at work today?
El trabajo va bien. | Work is going well.
¡Buen trabajo! | Good job!
Necesito dos trabajos para pagar la renta. | I need two jobs to pay the rent.
Él tiene tres trabajos para mantener a su familia. | He has three jobs to support his family.
Mis trabajos anteriores fueron en ventas. | My previous jobs were in sales.
Los trabajos temporales no dan prestaciones. | Temporary jobs don't provide benefits.

14 – dinero | **money**

Necesito dinero para pagar la renta. | I need money to pay the rent.
No tengo suficiente dinero. | I don't have enough money.
Gasté todo mi dinero. | I spent all my money.
El dinero no compra la felicidad. | Money doesn't buy happiness.
No todo se puede comprar con dinero. | Not everything can be bought with money.
Mis padres me dejaron dinero cuando fallecieron. | My parents left me money when they passed away.
El dinero no lo es todo. | Money isn't everything.
Hay cosas más importantes que el dinero. | There are things more important than money.
El tiempo es dinero. | Time is money.
El dinero no crece en los árboles. | Money doesn't grow on trees.

15 – familia | **family**

Sin familia, la vida es vacía. | Without family, life is empty.
La familia es lo más importante. | Family is the most important thing.
Mi familia siempre me apoya. | My family always supports me.
Viajamos en familia cada verano. | We travel as a family every summer.
La familia se reunió en la casa de mi abuela. | The family gathered at my grandma's house.
Toda la familia está invitada a la boda. | The whole family is invited to the wedding.
Las familias de los alumnos asistieron al evento. | The students' families attended the event.
Las familias del barrio organizaron una fiesta. | The neighborhood families organized a party.
Las familias mexicanas suelen ser grandes. | Mexican families tend to be large.
Varias familias viven en este edificio. | Several families live in this building.

16 – problema	**problem**
¿Cuál es el problema?	What's the problem?
Hay un problema con la entrega.	There's a problem with the delivery.
Ese no es mi problema.	That's not my problem.
No es un problema grave.	It's not a serious problem.
No te preocupes, todo problema tiene una solución.	Don't worry, every problem has a solution.
No quiero que esto se convierta en un problema.	I don't want this to become a problem.
Tu problema es que siempre llegas tarde.	Your problem is that you're always late.
No pensé que fuera un problema tan grande.	I didn't think it was such a big problem.
Tengo muchos problemas con el internet hoy.	I'm having a lot of problems with the internet today.
Los problemas entre ellos vienen de hace años.	The problems between them go back years.

17 – nombre	**name**
¿Cuál es tu nombre?	What is your name?
Mi nombre es ...	My name is ...
Perdón, olvidé tu nombre.	Sorry, I forgot your name.
¿Cómo se escribe tu nombre?	How is your name spelled?
Ella cambió su nombre cuando se casó.	She changed her name when she got married.
¿A nombre de quién está la reserva?	Under whose name is the reservation?
No encuentro tu nombre en la lista.	I can't find your name on the list.
Los profesores tienen que recordar muchos nombres.	Teachers have to remember a lot of names.
Los nombres de mis hijos son Juan y María.	My children's names are Juan and María.
Me gustan los nombres tradicionales.	I like traditional names.

18 – lugar	**place, spot**
Este lugar es perfecto para la boda.	This place is perfect for the wedding.
Estoy buscando un lugar tranquilo para leer.	I'm looking for a quiet place to read.
¿Conoces un buen lugar para comer?	Do you know a good place to eat?
Este lugar es muy bonito.	This place is really nice.
Te guardamos un lugar.	We saved you a spot.
Terminé en segundo lugar.	I finished in second place.
Me siento fuera de lugar.	I feel out of place.
Es un lugar difícil de olvidar.	It's a hard place to forget.
¿Por qué compraste una moto en lugar de un carro?	Why did you buy a motorcycle instead of a car?
Es uno de mis lugares favoritos.	It's one of my favorite places.

19 – momento | **moment**

Fue un momento especial. | It was a special moment.
Espera un momento, ya regreso. | Wait a moment, I'll be right back.
Dame un momento, por favor. | Give me a moment, please.
Fue el mejor momento de mi vida. | It was the best moment of my life.
Quiero recordar este momento para siempre. | I want to remember this moment forever.
Llegó el momento de decidir. | The time has come to decide.
Este es el mejor momento para hacerlo. | This is the best time to do it.
Desde el momento en que te vi, supe que eras especial. | From the moment I saw you, I knew you were special.
Pasamos momentos muy difíciles el año pasado. | We went through very difficult times last year.
Hubo momentos de tensión durante la reunión. | There were tense moments during the meeting.

20 – hombre | **man**

¿Quién es ese hombre? | Who is that man?
No conozco a ese hombre. | I don't know that man.
Ese hombre es mi esposo. | That man is my husband.
Mi padre es un hombre trabajador. | My father is a hardworking man.
Un hombre vino a buscarte. | A man came looking for you.
A los hombres les gusta asar carne y tomar cerveza. | Men like to grill meat and drink beer.
Cuatro hombres pintaron mi casa en una semana. | Four men painted my house in a week.
Vi a dos hombres discutiendo en la calle. | I saw two men arguing on the street.
Los hombres estaban bebiendo cerveza en el bar. | The men were drinking beer at the bar.
Esos hombres son muy peligrosos. | Those men are very dangerous.

21 – mujer | **woman, wife**

Esa mujer es mi vecina. | That woman is my neighbor.
Mi mujer y yo vamos al cine hoy. | My wife and I are going to the movies today.
¿Conoces a la mujer que vive en el tercer piso? | Do you know the woman who lives on the third floor?
Esa mujer sabe perfectamente lo que está haciendo. | That woman knows exactly what she's doing.
La mujer desapareció sin dejar rastro. | The woman disappeared without a trace.
Las mujeres suelen vivir más que los hombres. | Women usually live longer than men.
Había muchas mujeres en la conferencia. | There were many women at the conference.
Las mujeres se fueron antes que los hombres. | The women left before the men.
Esas mujeres son amigas. | Those women are friends.
Las mujeres están platicando. | The women are chatting.

22 – mano | **hand**

Levanta la mano si tienes una pregunta. | Raise your hand if you have a question.
Está hecho a mano. | It's handmade.
¿Cómo te lastimaste la mano? | How did you hurt your hand?
Mis abuelos caminan tomados de la mano. | My grandparents walk holding hands.
¿Me echas una mano con esto? | Will you give me a hand with this?
Dame la mano mientras cruzamos la calle. | Give me your hand while we cross the street.
Lávate las manos antes de comer. | Wash your hands before eating.
Las manos del bebé son pequeñitas. | The baby's hands are tiny.
Mis manos siempre están frías. | My hands are always cold.
Mis manos se resecan mucho en el invierno. | My hands get really dry in the winter.

23 – agua | **water**

¿Quieres un poco de agua? | Do you want some water?
Toma agua, hace mucho calor. | Drink some water, it's really hot.
Tomo agua durante todo el día. | I drink water throughout the day.
No tomes tanta agua antes de acostarte. | Don't drink too much water before going to bed.
El agua de llave en México sabe a cloro. | The tap water in Mexico tastes like chlorine.
El agua hierve a cien grados centígrados. | Water boils at one hundred degrees Celsius.
La gente no puede vivir mucho tiempo sin agua. | People can't live long without water.
Se acabó el agua caliente. | The hot water ran out.
Las aguas residuales deben limpiarse. | Wastewater must be cleaned.
¡Aguas! | Watch out!

24 – hora | **hour, time**

¿Qué hora es? | What time is it?
Ya casi es hora de irnos. | It's almost time for us to go.
Media hora es suficiente para llegar. | Half an hour is enough to get there.
¿A qué hora sales del trabajo? | What time do you leave work?
¿Cuántas horas duermes? | How many hours do you sleep?
Duermo ocho horas. | I sleep eight hours.
No hay suficientes horas en el día. | There aren't enough hours in the day.
Las horas volaron como minutos. | Hours flew by like minutes.
Las horas extras se pagan doble. | Overtime hours are paid double.
Pasé horas en el tráfico. | I spent hours in traffic.

25 – calle | **street**

Vivo en esta calle. | I live on this street.
La calle está cerrada. | The street is closed.
Dobla en la siguiente calle. | Turn at the next street.
Hay mucho tráfico en esa calle. | There's a lot of traffic on that street.
Los niños están jugando fútbol en la calle. | The kids are playing soccer in the street.
Esta es mi calle favorita porque huele a tacos. | This is my favorite street because it smells like tacos.
Las calles viejas tienen mucho encanto. | Old streets have a lot of charm.
Anduvimos por las calles buscando un café. | We wandered through the streets looking for a café.
Las calles se inundan cuando llueve mucho. | The streets flood when it rains a lot.
Cerraron las calles por el desfile. | They closed the streets for the parade.

26 – mañana | **morning**

Disfruto la paz de la mañana. | I enjoy the peace of the morning.
Disfruto el olor del café por la mañana. | I enjoy the smell of coffee in the morning.
Pasamos la mañana limpiando la casa. | We spent the morning cleaning the house.
Dedico la mañana a escribir. | I dedicate the morning to writing.
Salí a correr temprano en la mañana. | I went running early in the morning.
No he comido desde la mañana. | I haven't eaten since morning.
Me gustan las mañanas soleadas. | I like sunny mornings.
Las mañanas son mejores con café. | Mornings are better with coffee.
Las mañanas de los sábados son mis favoritas. | Saturday mornings are my favorite.
Odio los lunes en la mañana. | I hate Monday mornings.

27 – noche | **night**

Pasé toda la noche estudiando. | I spent all night studying.
Recordaré esta noche para siempre. | I'll remember this night forever.
No salgas solo por la noche. | Don't go out alone at night.
Este barrio no es seguro por la noche. | This neighborhood isn't safe at night.
Esta noche vamos al cine. | Tonight we're going to the movies.
Se hace de noche temprano en invierno. | It gets dark early in the winter.
Buenas noches a todos. | Good night, everyone.
No he dormido bien las últimas tres noches. | I haven't slept well the last three nights.
Las noches en el desierto son frías. | Nights in the desert are cold.
Me encantan los viernes por la noche. | I love Friday nights.

28 – caso | **case, instance, situation**

Es un caso especial. | It's a special case.
Llevo dinero extra en caso de emergencia. | I carry extra money in case of an emergency.
En ese caso, mejor nos vamos ahora. | In that case, we'd better leave now.
En todo caso, gracias por venir. | In any case, thanks for coming.
El abogado ganó el caso. | The lawyer won the case.
En estos casos, es mejor callar. | In these cases, it's better to stay quiet.
En el peor de los casos, perdemos un poco de dinero. | In the worst-case scenario, we lose a little money.
En todos los casos, es mejor preguntar. | In all cases, it's better to ask.
Hay casos de gripe en el colegio. | There are flu cases at school.
Hubo tres casos esta semana. | There were three cases this week.

29 – ciudad | **city**

¿De qué ciudad eres? | What city are you from?
Mi ciudad natal es Guanajuato. | My hometown is Guanajuato.
Me encanta vivir en la ciudad. | I love living in the city.
Esta ciudad nunca descansa. | This city never rests.
La ciudad está llena de turistas. | The city is full of tourists.
No aguanto el ruido de la ciudad. | I can't stand the city's noise.
Visitamos varias ciudades españolas. | We visited several Spanish cities.
Mis ciudades favoritas fueron Sevilla y Granada. | My favorite cities were Sevilla and Granada.
Me gustan las ciudades con historia. | I like cities with history.
Las ciudades se fundan cerca de cuerpos de agua. | Cities are founded near bodies of water.

30 – comida | **food, meal**

¿Te gusta la comida picante? | Do you like spicy food?
Me encanta la comida mexicana. | I love Mexican food.
La comida huele delicioso. | The food smells delicious.
Esa comida valió cada peso. | That food was worth every peso.
La comida de mi abuela es deliciosa. | My grandmother's food is delicious.
Su comida une a la familia. | Her food brings the family together.
La comida rápida no es saludable. | Fast food isn't healthy.
Compramos comida para la semana. | We bought food for the week.
Dos comidas grandes al día son suficientes para mí. | Two big meals a day is enough for me.
Prefiero cuatro comidas pequeñas. | I prefer four small meals.

31 – hijo, hija — **son, daughter**

Tu hijo se parece mucho a ti. — Your son looks a lot like you.
Es hijo único y es muy consentido. — He's an only child and is very spoiled.
Mi hijo menor adora a su abuelo. — My youngest son adores his grandfather.
Tengo una hija que ama los gatos. — I have a daughter who loves cats.
Mi hija se casó el mes pasado. — My daughter got married last month.
Mi hija me ayudó a cocinar. — My daughter helped me cook.
Amo a mis hijos con todo mi corazón. — I love my kids with all my heart.
¿Cuántos hijos tienes? — How many children do you have?
Mis hijas comparten cuarto. — My daughters share a room.
Tengo dos hijas y un hijo. — I have two daughters and one son.

32 – clase — **class**

La clase empieza a las ocho. — Class starts at eight.
La clase tiene veinte estudiantes. — The class has twenty students.
¿A qué hora termina la clase? — What time does the class end?
Esta clase pasa volando, es muy interesante. — This class flies by, it's very interesting.
Nunca he volado en primera clase. — I've never flown first class.
Es un hotel de clase mundial. — It's a world-class hotel.
Ya acabé mis clases por hoy. — I've finished my classes for today.
Las clases en línea son convenientes. — Online classes are convenient.
No me gustan las clases en línea. — I don't like online classes.
Me gustan más las clases presenciales. — I like in-person classes better.

33 – país — **country**

¿De qué país eres? — What country are you from?
Quiero mudarme a otro país. — I want to move to another country.
Canadá es un país frío pero hermoso. — Canada is a cold but beautiful country.
España es el país de mis ancestros. — Spain is the country of my ancestors.
Necesitas pasaporte para salir del país. — You need a passport to leave the country.
He visitado muchos países. — I've visited many countries.
He estado en quince países. — I have been to fifteen countries.
Visitamos tres países en este viaje. — We visited three countries on this trip.
Este es uno de mis países favoritos para visitar. — This is one of my favorite countries to visit.
Esos países han estado en guerra desde hace años. — Those countries have been at war for years.

34 – grupo

Formaron un grupo para estudiar juntos.
Estudiar en grupo no es para mí.
Me gusta mucho ese grupo musical.
El grupo se disolvió hace años.
El grupo se reúne todos los lunes.
Nuestro grupo ganó el primer lugar.
Los grupos musicales tocan en el festival.
Dividimos la clase en grupos pequeños.
Los grupos presentaron sus proyectos.
Dividieron a los grupos por edad.

group

They formed a group to study together.
Studying in a group isn't for me.
I really like that music group.
The group broke up years ago.
The group meets every Monday.
Our group won first place.
The musical groups play at the festival.
We divided the class into small groups.
The groups presented their projects.
They divided the groups by age.

35 – punto

Cada pregunta vale un punto.
El partido se decidió por un solo punto.
Estoy a punto de salir de la casa.
Ya estamos a punto de terminar.
No entendí tu punto de vista.
Desde mi punto de vista, deberías aceptar esa oferta.
Cada punto de luz en el cielo es una estrella.
Necesito mejorar mis puntos débiles.
Tenemos puntos de vista diferentes sobre ese tema.
¿Cuáles son los puntos más importantes de la reunión?

point

Each question is worth one point.
The game was decided by a single point.
I'm about to leave the house.
We're about to finish.
I didn't understand your point of view.
From my point of view, you should accept that offer.
Every point of light in the sky is a star.
I need to improve my weak points.
We have different points of view on that topic.
What are the most important points from the meeting?

36 – niño, niña

Mi niño quiere ser astronauta.
Ponme atención, niño.
Ese niño es maleducado.
La niña pidió un cuento antes de dormir.
La hija menor de los vecinos es una niña preciosa.
Esa niña parece vivir en su propio mundo.
Los niños pequeños tienen mucha energía.
Los niños se fueron al cine con su papá.
Las niñas están jugando afuera.
¿Esas niñas son hermanas?

child, boy, girl

My boy wants to be an astronaut.
Pay attention to me, boy.
That boy is rude.
The girl asked for a story before bed.
The neighbors' youngest daughter is a lovely girl.
That girl seems to live in her own world.
Little boys have a lot of energy.
The boys went to the movies with their dad.
The girls are playing outside.
Are those girls sisters?

37 – manera | **way, manner**

Él habla de manera clara y directa. | He speaks in a clear and direct way.
Me gusta tu manera de pensar. | I like your way of thinking.
Lo hizo de manera inteligente. | He did it in an intelligent way.
Hazlo a tu manera si quieres. | Do it your way if you want.
La manera como lo dijo fue ofensiva. | The way he said it was offensive.
No me gusta la manera en que me trata. | I don't like the way he treats me.
Ella tiene una manera muy dulce de tratar a la gente. | She has a very sweet way of treating people.
Esa no es manera de tratar a una persona. | That's no way to treat a person.
Esa es una buena manera de solucionarlo. | That's a good way to solve it.
Hay varias maneras de hacerlo. | There are several ways to do this.

38 – historia | **story, history**

Esa película está basada en una historia real. | That movie is based on a true story.
La historia que me contaste me hizo llorar. | The story you told me made me cry.
Es la historia de mi vida. | It's the story of my life.
Estudié historia en la universidad. | I studied history at university.
Aprendemos mucho de la historia. | We learn a lot from history.
La historia se repite. | History repeats itself.
Las historias que escribe son muy buenas. | The stories he writes are very good.
No todas las historias tienen final feliz. | Not all stories have a happy ending.
Ella siempre me cuenta las mismas historias. | She always tells me the same stories.
He leído muchas historias como esa. | I've read many stories like that.

39 – mes | **month**

Cada mes pago la renta el primer día. | Each month I pay the rent on the first day.
Voy a renunciar a fin de mes. | I'm going to quit at the end of the month.
El próximo mes empiezo mi nuevo trabajo. | Next month I start my new job.
Este mes ha pasado muy rápido. | This month has gone by really fast.
El mes pasado llovió casi todos los días. | Last month it rained almost every day.
Me pagan dos veces por mes. | They pay me two times per month.
Cada seis meses visito al dentista. | Every six months I visit the dentist.
Tengo tres meses de embarazo. | I'm three months pregnant.
La mayoría de los meses tienen treinta y un días. | Most months have 31 days.
Los meses de verano son muy calientes aquí. | The summer months are very hot here.

40 – amigo, amiga

friend

Mi mejor amigo vive en otra ciudad. — My best friend lives in another city.
Es un amigo de la infancia. — He's a childhood friend.
Un amigo de verdad no te juzga. — A true friend doesn't judge you.
Tengo una amiga que siempre me escucha. — I have a friend who always listens to me.
Es más que una amiga, es como mi hermana. — She's more than a friend, she's like my sister.
Mi amiga viene a visitarme mañana. — My friend is coming to visit me tomorrow.
Hice muchos amigos en el colegio. — I made many friends at school.
Voy al cine con unos amigos. — I'm going to the movies with some friends.
Mis amigas organizaron la fiesta. — My friends organized the party.
Salgo con mis amigas los viernes. — I go out with my friends on Fridays.

41 – padre, papá

father, dad

La gente dice que me parezco mucho a mi padre. — People say I look a lot like my father.
Mi padre cuenta las mejores historias. — My father tells the best stories.
Mi padre es viejo pero todavía está sano. — My father is old but still healthy.
Jamás he visto a un padre tan paciente. — I've never seen a father so patient.
Espero ser un buen papá. — I hope I'll be a good dad.
A nuestro papá le encanta bailar. — Our dad loves to dance.
Mi papá es estricto, pero también es divertido. — My dad is strict, but he's also fun.
Mis padres vienen de visita. — My parents are coming to visit.
Tus papás viajan mucho. — Your parents travel a lot.
¿Te gustaría conocer a mis papás? — Would you like to meet my parents?

42 – madre, mamá

mother, mom

Su madre trabaja en un hospital. — His mother works at a hospital.
Toda madre merece respeto. — Every mother deserves respect.
¿Dónde está mi mamá? — Where is my mom?
Mamá, ¿me ayudas con la tarea? — Mom, can you help me with my homework?
Mi mamá se preocupa cuando llego tarde a casa. — My mom worries when I come home late.
Mi mamá cuida a mis hijos una vez por semana. — My mom watches my kids once per week.
Mi mamá es mi mejor amiga. — My mom is my best friend.
El Día de las Madres es en mayo. — Mother's Day is in May.
Las madres parecen tener una paciencia infinita. — Mothers seem to have endless patience.
Nuestras madres se conocen bien. — Our mothers know each other well.

43 – amor

love

¿Crees en el amor a primera vista? — Do you believe in love at first sight?
El amor a primera vista sí existe. — Love at first sight does exist.
Me casé con el amor de mi juventud. — I married the love of my youth.
Él es el amor de mi vida. — He's the love of my life.
Te extraño mucho, mi amor. — I miss you so much, my love.
El amor es más fuerte que el odio. — Love is stronger than hate.
No confundas el deseo con el amor. — Don't confuse desire with love.
El amor de madre es incondicional. — A mother's love is unconditional.
Él hizo todo por amor a su familia. — He did everything out of love for his family.
Los amores de verano no suelen durar. — Summer loves don't usually last.

44 – cabeza

head

Me duele la cabeza. — My head hurts.
Tengo dolor de cabeza. — I have a headache.
Ella tiene cabeza para los números. — She has a head for numbers.
Ella se lanzó de cabeza a la piscina. — She dove headfirst into the pool.
No te lances de cabeza al río. — Don't dive headfirst into the river.
Sus amigos le meten malas ideas en la cabeza. — His friends put bad ideas in his head.
Sin querer, me pegué en la cabeza con la mesa. — I accidentally hit my head on the table.
El perro sacó la cabeza por la ventana. — The dog stuck his head out the window.
No puedo sacarme esa canción de la cabeza. — I can't get that song out of my head.
Dos cabezas piensan mejor que una. — Two heads think better than one.

45 – corazón

heart

Mi corazón late muy rápido cuando corro. — My heart beats very fast when I run.
Ella me rompió el corazón. — She broke my heart.
Gracias de todo corazón. — Thank you from the bottom of my heart.
Mi madre tiene un corazón de oro. — My mother has a heart of gold.
Se me partió el corazón verla llorar. — It broke my heart to see her cry.
No tengo corazón para decirle que no. — I don't have the heart to tell him no.
Dibujé un corazón en la tarjeta para mi mamá. — I drew a heart on the card for my mom.
Mi abuela tiene problemas del corazón. — My grandmother has heart problems.
El doctor escuchó mi corazón con el estetoscopio. — The doctor listened to my heart with the stethoscope.
Nuestros corazones laten como uno solo. — Our hearts beat as one.

46 – hermano, hermana
Tengo un hermano mayor.
Mi hermano y yo somos muy diferentes.
Siempre peleo con mi hermano.
Tengo una hermana menor.
A mi hermana le encantan los gatos.
¿Tu hermana está saliendo con alguien?
¿Tienes hermanos?
Mis hermanos siempre me molestan.
Mis hermanas no se llevan bien.
Mis hermanas se parecen muchísimo.

brother, sister
I have an older brother.
My brother and I are very different.
I always fight with my brother.
I have a younger sister.
My sister loves cats.
Is your sister dating anyone?
Do you have siblings?
My brothers always bother me.
My sisters do not get along well.
My sisters look very much alike.

47 – muerte
La muerte es parte natural de la vida.
Nadie puede escapar de la muerte.
No quiero hablar de la muerte.
La muerte de mi tío nos tomó por sorpresa.
Le temo más al dolor que a la muerte.
La muerte de su perro lo dejó muy triste.
La muerte del actor sorprendió a todos.
Hubo varias muertes en el accidente.
La ola de calor causó varias muertes.
Las muertes fueron evitables.

death
Death is a natural part of life.
No one can escape death.
I don't want to talk about death.
My uncle's death took us by surprise.
I fear pain more than death.
His dog's death left him very sad.
The actor's death surprised everyone.
There were several deaths in the accident.
The heat wave caused several deaths.
The deaths were preventable.

48 – señor, señora
Buenos días, señor.
Señor, su mesa está lista.
El Sr. Ramírez está aquí para la entrevista.
Buenas tardes, señora.
La señora vive sola con sus gatos.
Conozco a la señora desde hace muchos años.
La señora García es mi profesora favorita.
Los señores de la mesa quieren la cuenta.
Señoras y señores, bienvenidos al evento.
Hola, señoras, ¿puedo ayudarlas en algo?

sir, ma'am
Good morning, sir.
Sir, your table is ready.
Mr. Ramirez is here for the interview.
Good afternoon, ma'am.
The lady lives alone with her cats.
I've known the lady for many years.
Ms. Garcia is my favorite teacher.
The men at the table want the check.
Ladies and gentlemen, welcome to the event.
Hello, ladies, may I help you with something?

49 – sangre | **blood**

Necesitamos más donantes de sangre. — We need more blood donors.
Donar sangre puede salvar vidas. — Donating blood can save lives.
Me mareo con solo ver sangre. — I get dizzy just from seeing blood.
Me desmayé al ver tanta sangre. — I fainted when I saw so much blood.
La sangre no dejaba de salir de la herida. — The blood wouldn't stop coming out of the wound.
Tuve una prueba de sangre esta mañana. — I had a blood test this morning.
Le sacaron sangre para hacerle unos exámenes. — They drew blood to run some tests.
Mi sangre estaba muy baja de hierro. — My blood was very low in iron.
Él tiene sangre mexicana por parte de su madre. — He has Mexican blood from his mother's side.
Me asusté cuando vi sangre en la camisa de mi hijo. — I got scared when I saw blood on my son's shirt.

50 – escuela | **school (general term, public)**

La escuela pública es gratuita. — Public school is free.
Ir a la escuela es obligatorio. — Going to school is mandatory.
No quiero faltar a la escuela mañana. — I don't want to miss school tomorrow.
No puedes ir a la escuela porque estás enfermo. — You can't go to school because you're sick.
Mañana no hay escuela. — There's no school tomorrow.
La escuela empieza a las ocho. — School starts at 8.
Dejé a los niños en la escuela. — I dropped the kids off at school.
Las escuelas públicas tienen muchos alumnos. — Public schools have many students.
Algunas escuelas cerraron por las fuertes lluvias. — Some schools closed because of the heavy rain.
Las escuelas rurales tienen pocos recursos. — Rural schools have few resources.

51 – mensaje | **message, text message**

Te mandé un mensaje de texto. — I sent you a text message.
Si no contesto, déjame un mensaje de voz. — Leave me a voice message if I don't answer.
Recibí tu mensaje esta mañana. — I received your message this morning.
No entendí el mensaje que me enviaste. — I didn't understand the message you sent me.
Mándame un mensaje cuando llegues. — Send me a message when you arrive.
El mensaje no se envió porque no había señal. — The message wasn't sent because there was no signal.
El mensaje de la película fue poderoso. — The movie's message was powerful.
¿Por qué no respondes mis mensajes? — Why don't you answer my messages?
No vi tus mensajes. — I didn't see your messages.
Borré todos mis mensajes. — I deleted all my messages.

52 – número | **number**

No tengo tu número. | I don't have your number.
¿Me das tu número? | Can you give me your number?
Mándame un mensaje para tener tu número. | Text me so I have your number.
Aquí está el número de orden. | Here's the order number.
¿Tienes el número de seguimiento? | Do you have the tracking number?
El dieciocho es mi número de la suerte. | Eighteen is my lucky number.
¿Qué número calzas? | What shoe size do you wear?
Los números pares son divisibles entre dos. | Even numbers are divisible by two.
¿Viste los números de la lotería? | Did you see the lottery numbers?
Solo tengo dos números de teléfono memorizados. | I only have two phone numbers memorized.

53 – sol | **sun**

Después de la lluvia, salió el sol. | After the rain, the sun came out.
Hoy hace mucho sol. | It's very sunny today.
Ponte bloqueador, está muy fuerte el sol. | Put on sunblock, the sun is very strong.
Me quemé con el sol. | I got sunburned.
El sol sale y el sol se pone. | The sun rises and the sun sets.
Los girasoles siguen al sol durante el día. | Sunflowers follow the sun during the day.
El sol desapareció detrás de las nubes. | The sun disappeared behind the clouds.
Vamos temprano antes de que salga el sol. | Let's go early before the sun comes out.
Cierra la cortina, entra mucho sol. | Close the curtain, too much sun is coming in.
El sol se refleja en el mar al atardecer. | The sun reflects on the ocean at sunset.

54 – ojo | **eye**

Se me metió algo en el ojo. | Something got in my eye.
Me duele el ojo desde ayer. | My eye has hurt since yesterday.
Mi papá perdió la vista de un ojo en un accidente. | My dad lost sight in one eye in an accident.
¡Ojo! El piso está mojado. | Careful! The floor is wet.
Cierra los ojos y pide un deseo. | Close your eyes and make a wish.
Me arden los ojos por el humo. | My eyes are burning from the smoke.
Ella tiene los ojos verdes como su mamá. | She has green eyes like her mom.
Mis ojos están cansados de tanto leer. | My eyes are tired from reading so much.
Se le llenaron los ojos de lágrimas. | Her eyes filled with tears.
El doctor me revisó los ojos con una luz. | The doctor examined my eyes with a light.

55 – lado

side

Estoy de tu lado.
I'm on your side.

Vivo del otro lado de la ciudad.
I live on the other side of the city.

El perro duerme a mi lado.
The dog sleeps beside me.

Mira el lado bueno.
Look on the bright side.

Me gusta más este lado de la cama.
I like this side of the bed better.

Estás en el lado equivocado de este tema.
You're on the wrong side of this issue.

Me salió el lado celoso cuando lo vi.
My jealous side came out when I saw him.

Te buscamos por todos lados.
We looked for you everywhere.

Los dos lados firmaron el acuerdo.
Both sides signed the agreement.

En el centro hay turistas por todos lados.
In downtown, there are tourists everywhere.

56 – mar

sea

Vivimos cerca del mar.
We live near the sea.

Mi casa tiene vista al mar.
My house has a sea view.

Escucho las olas del mar todas las noches.
I hear the waves of the sea every night.

El sonido del mar me duerme.
The sound of the sea puts me to sleep.

Nada me relaja más que el mar.
Nothing relaxes me more than the sea.

Hay muchos peces en el mar.
There are many fish in the sea.

El mar Mediterráneo tiene mucha historia.
The Mediterranean Sea has a lot of history.

Solo nado en el mar si el agua está cálida y cristalina.
I only swim in the sea if the water is warm and clear.

Prefiero el mar a la piscina.
I prefer the sea to the pool.

Los mares del norte son muy fríos.
The northern seas are very cold.

57 – luz

light

Prende la luz.
Turn on the light.

Apaga la luz.
Turn off the light.

Necesitamos más luz en esta habitación.
We need more light in this room.

La luz se cortó por la tormenta.
The power went out because of the storm.

Las calles con más luz son más seguras de noche.
Streets with more light are safer at night.

Más luz significa más seguridad.
More light means more security.

La luz del faro guía a los barcos.
The light from the lighthouse guides the ships.

Las luces de la ciudad son visibles desde el espacio.
The city lights are visible from space.

Las luces del árbol se ven hermosas.
The lights on the tree look beautiful.

Las luces del carro quedaron prendidas.
The car lights were left on.

58 – cuerpo | **body**

El ejercicio es bueno para el cuerpo. | Exercise is good for the body.
El cuerpo humano tiene más de doscientos huesos. | The human body has over two hundred bones.
Cuida tu cuerpo con buena alimentación. | Take care of your body with good nutrition.
Me duele el cuerpo después de hacer ejercicio. | My body is sore after exercising.
Necesito escuchar a mi cuerpo. | I need to listen to my body.
Me duele todo el cuerpo. | My whole body hurts.
Encontraron el cuerpo en el río. | They found the body in the river.
Los cuerpos fueron encontrados esta mañana. | The bodies were found this morning.
Los cuerpos estaban cubiertos con mantas. | The bodies were covered with blankets.
Ya identificaron los cuerpos. | They already identified the bodies.

59 – teléfono | **telephone, phone**

¿Dónde dejé mi teléfono? | Where did I leave my phone?
Dejaste el teléfono cargando en la cocina. | You left the phone charging in the kitchen.
No escuché sonar el teléfono. | I didn't hear the phone ring.
¿Cuál es tu número de teléfono? | What is your phone number?
Ella me habló por teléfono. | She called me on the phone.
Mi abuelo todavía tiene teléfono fijo. | My grandpa still has a landline.
Hablamos por teléfono ayer. | We talked on the phone yesterday.
Apaguen sus teléfonos. | Turn off your phones.
Los teléfonos públicos ya casi no existen. | Public phones hardly exist anymore.
Los teléfonos solían tener cables. | Telephones used to have cords.

60 – cara | **face**

Él se lavó la cara antes de irse a dormir. | He washed his face before going to sleep.
Me duele la cara de tanto reír. | My face hurts from laughing so much.
Su cara se puso roja de vergüenza. | Her face turned red with embarrassment.
La niña escondió su cara entre las manos. | The girl hid her face in her hands.
La cara de mi abuela está llena de arrugas. | My grandmother's face is full of wrinkles.
Tu perro tiene una cara muy expresiva. | Your dog has a very expressive face.
Recuerdo tu cara, pero no tu nombre. | I remember your face but not your name.
Los humanos somos buenos reconociendo caras. | Humans are good at recognizing faces.
Los niños se están haciendo caras. | The kids are making faces at each other.
Vi muchas caras conocidas en la fiesta. | I saw many familiar faces at the party.

61 – semana | **week**

Esta semana tengo mucho trabajo. — This week I have a lot of work.
La semana comenzó con buenas noticias. — The week began with good news.
Nos vemos la próxima semana. — See you next week.
Esta semana llovió casi todos los días. — It rained almost every day this week.
He dormido mal toda la semana. — I've slept badly all week.
Las últimas semanas han sido difíciles. — The last few weeks have been difficult.
Habrá cambios en las próximas semanas. — There will be changes in the coming weeks.
Mis hijos estuvieron enfermos por dos semanas. — My kids were sick for two weeks.
He estado muy cansado estas últimas semanas. — I've been really tired these past few weeks.
No nos hemos visto en semanas. — We haven't seen each other in weeks.

62 – tierra | **earth, land, ground, soil, dirt**

Esta tierra es muy fértil. — This soil is very fertile.
La tierra está muy seca por falta de lluvia. — The ground is very dry from lack of rain.
La tierra se volvió lodo con la lluvia. — The ground turned into mud from the rain.
La tierra tiembla durante los terremotos. — The ground shakes during earthquakes.
¿Por qué el perro está cubierto de tierra? — Why is the dog covered in dirt?
La tierra gira alrededor del sol. — The Earth revolves around the sun.
Los agricultores preparan la tierra para sembrar. — The farmers prepare the soil for planting.
Las tierras bajas se inundan fácilmente. — The lowlands flood easily.
Mis abuelos tienen muchas tierras en el norte. — My grandparents have a lot of land in the north.
Trabajan las tierras desde el amanecer. — They work the lands from dawn.

63 – palabra | **word**

Te doy mi palabra. — I give you my word.
Él cumplió su palabra como prometió. — He kept his word as he promised.
Es un hombre de palabra. — He's a man of his word.
"Amor" es una palabra común en español. — "Love" is a common word in Spanish.
La palabra "amor" tiene cuatro letras. — The word "amor" has four letters.
¿Es esa la palabra correcta? — Is that the right word?
Ella escogió sus palabras cuidadosamente. — She chose her words carefully.
Las palabras tienen mucho poder. — Words have a lot of power.
Tus palabras me lastimaron mucho. — Your words hurt me a lot.
Intento aprender diez palabras nuevas cada día. — I try to learn ten new words each day.

64 – ejemplo

example

Dame un ejemplo sencillo.
Give me a simple example.

Hay muchas frutas ricas, por ejemplo, el mango.
There are many tasty fruits, for example, mango.

Ese caso fue un claro ejemplo de corrupción.
That case was a clear example of corruption.

Él da mal ejemplo cuando grita así.
He sets a bad example when he yells like that.

Ella sirve de ejemplo para los demás estudiantes.
She serves as an example for the other students.

Dar el ejemplo es más efectivo que dar consejos.
Setting an example is more effective than giving advice.

Aprendo mejor viendo ejemplos.
I learn better by seeing examples.

¿Tienes más ejemplos?
Do you have more examples?

Estoy buscando ejemplos prácticos.
I'm looking for practical examples.

Los ejemplos que diste fueron perfectos.
The examples you gave were perfect.

65 – carro

car

¿Tienes carro?
Do you have a car?

¿Se necesita carro en esta ciudad?
Is a car needed in this city?

Mi carro está en el taller.
My car is in the shop.

Casi nunca lavo mi carro.
I hardly ever wash my car.

Mis papás me regalaron este carro.
My parents gave me this car as a gift.

El carro es viejo, pero funciona muy bien.
The car is old, but it runs great.

Muchos carros ya no usan gasolina.
Many cars no longer use gasoline.

Los carros eléctricos son silenciosos.
Electric cars are quiet.

Los carros están subiendo de precio cada año.
Cars are getting more expensive every year.

Los carros de hoy tienen mucha tecnología.
Today's cars have lots of technology.

66 – minuto

minute

Perdí el tren por un minuto.
I missed the train by one minute.

Dame un minuto para pensarlo.
Give me a minute to think about it.

El estadio entero guardó un minuto de silencio.
The entire stadium observed a minute of silence.

¿Tienes un minuto para hablar?
Do you have a minute to talk?

Espera un minuto.
Wait a minute.

Quedan cinco minutos antes de que suene la campana.
Five minutes left before the bell rings.

El partido mantuvo la emoción durante noventa minutos.
The game was ninety minutes of non-stop excitement.

Vuelvo en diez minutos.
I'll be back in ten minutes.

Todo cambió en cuestión de minutos.
Everything changed in a matter of minutes.

La cena estará lista en cinco minutos.
Dinner will be ready in five minutes.

67 – libro	**book**
¿Ya terminaste el libro?	Did you finish the book yet?
El libro es muy interesante.	The book is very interesting.
Ese libro me cambió la forma de pensar.	That book changed the way I think.
Me gusta leer un libro antes de dormir.	I like to read a book before sleeping.
Me dormí leyendo el libro.	I fell asleep while reading the book.
No juzgues un libro por su portada.	Don't judge a book by its cover.
Tengo muchos libros en mi cuarto.	I have many books in my room.
Vendí mis libros viejos.	I sold my old books.
Los libros digitales son más baratos.	Digital books are cheaper.
No me gusta leer libros en una pantalla.	I don't like reading books on a screen.

68 – pregunta	**question**
Tengo una pregunta.	I have a question.
¿Puedo hacerte una pregunta?	Can I ask you a question?
Buena pregunta.	Good question.
Tu pregunta no tiene una respuesta sencilla.	Your question doesn't have an easy answer.
No entendí la pregunta.	I didn't understand the question.
Mis hijos hacen preguntas interesantes.	My children ask interesting questions.
Si tienes más preguntas, avísame.	If you have more questions, let me know.
Las preguntas del examen estuvieron complicadas.	The test questions were tricky.
Contesté todas las preguntas.	I answered all the questions.
Me hicieron muchas preguntas en la entrevista.	They asked me many questions in the interview.

69 – puerta	**door**
Alguien tocó la puerta.	Someone knocked on the door.
¿Puedes abrir la puerta, por favor?	Can you open the door, please?
Dejé la puerta abierta por accidente.	I left the door open by accident.
La puerta está abierta, ciérrala por favor.	The door is open, close it please.
Cerré la puerta porque hacía frío.	I closed the door because it was cold.
Toqué la puerta, pero nadie respondió.	I knocked on the door, but no one answered.
La puerta del baño no cierra bien.	The bathroom door doesn't close properly.
¿Ya cerraste las puertas del carro?	Did you already lock the car doors?
Las puertas del edificio son automáticas.	The building's doors are automatic.
Este trabajo me abrió muchas puertas en mi carrera.	This job opened many doors for me in my career.

70 – baño | **bathroom, bath**

Necesito ir al baño ya. | I need to go to the bathroom now.
¿Dónde está el baño? | Where is the bathroom?
El baño está al fondo. | The bathroom is at the back.
¿Puedo usar tu baño? | Can I use your bathroom?
Ese baño no tiene papel. | That bathroom has no toilet paper.
Cerraron el baño para limpiarlo. | They closed the bathroom in order to clean it.
El perro necesita un baño. | The dog needs a bath.
El bebé se durmió después del baño caliente. | The baby fell asleep after the warm bath.
Los baños están cerrados. | The bathrooms are closed.
¿Dónde están los baños públicos? | Where are the public restrooms?

71 – celular | **cell phone**

Olvidé mi celular en el carro. | I forgot my cell phone in the car.
Siempre estoy pegado al celular. | I'm always glued to my phone.
Dejé mi celular cargando en la otra habitación. | I left my phone charging in the other room.
Se me cayó el celular y se rompió la pantalla. | I dropped my cell phone and the screen broke.
¿Mi celular funcionará en este país? | Will my phone work in this country?
El abuelo todavía no tiene celular. | Grandpa still doesn't have a cell phone.
Ya todos los niños tienen celulares. | All the kids have phones now.
Los celulares deben estar apagados en los cines. | Cell phones must be turned off in movie theaters.
Los celulares están prohibidos en clase. | Cell phones are prohibited in class.
No pueden usar los celulares en clase. | You can't use phones in class.

72 – llave | **key, faucet**

Intenté abrir la puerta y se rompió la llave. | I tried to open the door, and the key broke.
Se partió la llave al girarla. | The key snapped when I turned it.
Te dejaré la llave debajo del tapete. | I'll leave you a key under the doormat.
Una buena educación es la llave que abre puertas. | A good education is the key that opens doors.
La llave del baño está goteando. | The bathroom faucet is dripping.
Intenté abrir la puerta con la llave equivocada. | I tried to open the door with the wrong key.
Dame las llaves, yo manejo. | Give me the keys, I'll drive.
Las llaves están sobre la mesa. | The keys are on the table.
Las llaves están en mi bolsa. | The keys are in my bag.
Ella copió las llaves sin que nadie supiera. | She copied the keys without anyone knowing.

73 – razón

Dame una razón para creerlo.
No hay razón para enojarse.
Tienes razón.
No veo una razón para cambiarlo.
No hay razón para preocuparse.
Entiendo la razón, pero no estoy de acuerdo.
Tengo mis razones para no querer ir a esa fiesta.
¿Cuáles son las razones de tu decisión?
Ella explicó sus razones con mucha calma.
No necesito explicarte mis razones.

reason

Give me a reason to believe it.
There's no reason to get upset.
You're right.
I don't see a reason to change it.
There's no reason to worry.
I understand the reason, but I don't agree.
I have my reasons for not wanting to go to that party.
What are the reasons for your decision?
She explained her reasons very calmly.
I don't need to explain my reasons to you.

74 – cama

Ya me voy a la cama.
Me quiero quedar en la cama.
La cama está muy cómoda.
No quiero salir de la cama.
A nuestros hijos les gusta saltar en nuestra cama.
Ella sigue en cama con fiebre.
Mis hijos hacen sus propias camas.
Mis abuelos duermen en camas separadas.
Todas las camas en Tanzania tienen mosquiteros.
Ese hotel es conocido por sus camas cómodas.

bed

I'm going to bed now.
I want to stay in bed.
The bed is really comfortable.
I don't want to get out of bed.
Our kids like to jump on our bed.
She's still in bed with a fever.
My kids make their own beds.
My grandparents sleep in separate beds.
All the beds in Tanzania have mosquito nets.
That hotel is known for its comfortable beds.

75 – mesa

Toda la comida está sobre la mesa.
Tomen asiento a la mesa.
¡Hora de comer! ¡Todos a la mesa!
Esta mesa está hecha a mano.
Mi bisabuelo hizo esta mesa hace noventa años.
Reservé una mesa para cuatro personas.
Te toca poner la mesa.
No caben todos en una sola mesa.
Necesitamos más mesas para la fiesta.
Juntaron las mesas para hacer una más larga.

table

All the food is on the table.
Take a seat at the table.
Time to eat! Everyone to the table!
This table is handmade.
My great-grandfather made this table 90 years ago.
I reserved a table for four people.
It's your turn to set the table.
Not everyone fits at just one table.
We need more tables for the party.
They pushed the tables together to make a longer one.

76 – ropa | **clothes, clothing**

Esa tienda tiene ropa muy bonita. | That store has really nice clothes.
La ropa está limpia, puedes guardarla. | The clothes are clean, you can put them away.
Se me acabó la ropa limpia. | I ran out of clean clothes.
Voy a donar la ropa que ya no uso. | I'm going to donate the clothes I don't use anymore.
Me gasté todo mi sueldo en ropa nueva. | I spent my whole paycheck on new clothes.
Lave la ropa nueva antes de usarla. | Wash new clothes before wearing them.
Con este calor, prefiero usar ropa ligera. | In this heat, I prefer to wear light clothing.
No tengo mucha ropa de invierno. | I don't have much winter clothing.
¿Por qué está toda tu ropa en el piso? | Why are all your clothes on the floor?
Mi abuela dobla la ropa mientras ve la tele. | My grandma folds the clothes while watching TV.

77 – tarde | **afternoon**

Quedamos de reunirnos a las cinco de la tarde. | We agreed to meet at five in the afternoon.
La tarde se ve hermosa hoy. | The afternoon looks beautiful today.
¿Estás disponible mañana por la tarde? | Are you available tomorrow afternoon?
¿Qué hiciste ayer en la tarde? | What did you do yesterday afternoon?
Pasé la mayor parte de la tarde en una librería. | I spent most of the afternoon at a bookstore.
Prefiero estudiar por la tarde, después de las clases. | I prefer to study in the afternoon after classes.
Siempre hay tráfico en la tarde. | There's always traffic in the afternoon.
Buenas tardes. | Good afternoon.
Hago ejercicio todas las tardes. | I exercise every afternoon.
Me encantan las tardes de domingo con la familia. | I love Sunday afternoons with the family.

78 – café | **coffee, café, coffee shop**

¿Vamos por un café? | Shall we go for a coffee?
¿Quieres leche en tu café? | Do you want milk in your coffee?
Prefiero el café sin azúcar. | I prefer coffee without sugar.
Me encanta el olor del café. | I love the smell of coffee.
Necesito mi café diario. | I need my daily coffee.
No puedo empezar el día sin un café. | I can't start the day without a coffee.
El mejor café es el de Colombia. | The best coffee is from Colombia.
Hay un café nuevo cerca de mi casa. | There is a new coffee shop near my house.
Nos vemos en el café de la esquina. | See you at the café on the corner.
Los cafés de esa zona son muy caros. | The cafés in that area are very expensive.

79 – empresa | **company**

Mi hermano trabaja en una empresa de tecnología. | My brother works at a tech company.
Él fundó su propia empresa hace tres años. | He founded his own company three years ago.
La empresa tiene más de cien empleados. | The company has more than a hundred employees.
La empresa expandió sus operaciones a Europa. | The company expanded its operations to Europe.
Trabajo en el departamento legal de la empresa. | I work in the company's legal department.
Esa empresa es nuestra principal competencia. | That company is our main competition.
Varias empresas patrocinan el evento. | Several companies are sponsoring the event.
Las empresas deben pagar impuestos justos. | Companies must pay fair taxes.
Las empresas grandes dominan el mercado. | Big companies dominate the market.
Las empresas locales crean empleos. | Local companies create jobs.

80 – centro | **center, downtown**

Voy al centro a ver a unos amigos. | I'm going downtown to see some friends.
El centro histórico está muy bonito. | The historic downtown is really nice.
No me gusta manejar en el centro. | I don't like driving downtown.
Hay mucho tráfico en el centro. | There's a lot of traffic downtown.
No hay dónde estacionarse en la calle en el centro. | There's nowhere to park on the street downtown.
Trabajo en el centro. | I work downtown.
En el centro deportivo dan clases gratis los sábados. | The sports center gives free classes on Saturdays.
Voy al centro de salud a vacunar a mi hijo. | I'm going to the health center to vaccinate my son.
La mayoría de los centros comerciales abren a las diez. | Most malls open at ten.
Los centros comerciales se llenan en Navidad. | Malls get packed at Christmas.

81 – precio | **price**

¿Cuál es el precio final? | What's the final price?
El precio incluye impuestos. | The price includes taxes.
¿Es el mejor precio que puede darme? | Is that the best price you can give me?
Yo no pagaría ese precio. | I wouldn't pay that price.
Me parece un precio justo. | It seems like a fair price to me.
El precio de la gasolina subió otra vez esta semana. | The price of gasoline went up again this week.
Hay mejores precios en línea. | There are better prices online.
Los precios en ese mercado son muy accesibles. | The prices in that market are very affordable.
Los precios son altos en ese restaurante. | The prices are high at that restaurant.
¿Por qué los precios son tan altos últimamente? | Why are prices so high lately?

82 – tienda | **store, shop**

¿A qué hora abre esa tienda? | What time does that store open?
La tienda abre a las nueve de la mañana. | The store opens at nine in the morning.
Mi mamá trabaja en una tienda de ropa. | My mom works in a clothing store.
Esa tienda vende ropa muy bonita. | That store sells very nice clothes.
Fui a la tienda a comprar leche. | I went to the store to buy milk.
La tienda cierra los domingos. | The store closes on Sundays.
Las tiendas en línea son muy populares ahora. | Online stores are very popular now.
Me gusta visitar tiendas de segunda mano. | I like visiting secondhand shops.
Hay muchas tiendas en ese centro comercial. | There are many stores in that mall.
Todas las tiendas cierran en Navidad. | All the stores close on Christmas.

83 – pan | **bread**

Voy a comprar el pan en la panadería. | I'm going to buy the bread at the bakery.
El pan de ese lugar es excelente. | The bread from that place is excellent.
Este pan integral es saludable. | This whole wheat bread is healthy.
Ese pan huele delicioso. | That bread smells delicious.
Necesito pan para hacer tortas. | I need bread to make sandwiches.
Hago pan en casa una vez por semana. | I make bread at home once per week.
El pan salió con una corteza perfecta. | The bread came out with a perfect crust.
Se nos acabó el pan. | We ran out of bread.
¿Puedes comprar pan en la tienda? | Can you buy bread at the store?
Los panes artesanales son más caros. | Artisanal breads are more expensive.

84 – leche | **milk**

Tomo leche todas las mañanas. | I drink milk every morning.
Necesito comprar leche en el supermercado. | I need to buy milk at the supermarket.
A los niños les encanta la leche con chocolate. | Kids love chocolate milk.
¿Quieres leche con tu café? | Do you want milk with your coffee?
La leche de vaca no me cae bien. | Cow's milk doesn't agree with me.
El bebé solo toma leche materna. | The baby only drinks breast milk.
Esa leche es sin lactosa. | That milk is lactose-free.
Las leches vegetales son muy populares ahora. | Plant-based milks are very popular now.
Las leches de almendra y coco son mis favoritas. | Almond and coconut milks are my favorites.
Las leches deslactosadas son más caras. | Lactose-free milks are more expensive.

85 – mercado | **market**

Hay un mercado pequeño cerca de mi casa. | There's a small market near my house.
El mercado está lleno de frutas frescas. | The market is full of fresh fruit.
Me encontré a mi tía en el mercado. | I ran into my aunt at the market.
El mercado cierra a las tres de la tarde. | The market closes at three in the afternoon.
Fui al mercado a comprar flores para mi abuela. | I went to the market to buy flowers for my grandma.
Mi mamá prefiere el mercado al supermercado. | My mom prefers the market over the supermarket.
Consigo todo más barato en el mercado. | I get everything cheaper at the market.
El mercado laboral es muy competitivo. | The job market is very competitive.
Me encanta caminar por los mercados al aire libre. | I love walking through open-air markets.
Los mercados están llenos de colores y aromas. | The markets are full of colors and aromas.

86 – televisión, televisor | **television, TV**

Ya no veo tanta televisión como antes. | I don't watch as much television as before.
El televisor no prende. | The television won't turn on.
Me dormí con el televisor prendido. | I fell asleep with the TV on.
Dejé el televisor prendido toda la noche. | I left the television on all night.
Mi abuela ve televisión todo el tiempo. | My grandmother watches television all the time.
Mi mamá no me deja ver televisión entre semana. | My mom doesn't let me watch TV during the week.
La televisión mexicana tiene buenas telenovelas. | Mexican television has good soap operas.
Compramos una tele nueva. | We bought a new TV.
Los televisores de ahora son muy delgados. | Televisions nowadays are very thin.
Las televisiones de esa marca duran muchos años. | TVs from that brand last for many years.

87 – fiesta | **party**

No hay fiesta sin música. | There's no party without music.
Esa fiesta fue inolvidable. | That party was unforgettable.
La fiesta terminó muy tarde. | The party ended very late.
Mis amigos van a hacer una fiesta esta noche. | My friends are going to throw a party tonight.
La fiesta empieza a las nueve de la noche. | The party starts at nine at night.
Nadie sabe a qué hora terminará la fiesta. | Nobody knows what time the party will end.
Conoces gente interesante en las fiestas. | You meet interesting people at parties.
Las fiestas de quince años cuestan una fortuna. | Quinceañera parties cost a fortune.
Las fiestas navideñas son mis favoritas. | Christmas parties are my favorite.
Mis padres no me dejan ir a fiestas. | My parents don't let me go to parties.

88 – aire

air

Necesito un poco de aire fresco.
I need some fresh air.

Abre la ventana para que entre aire fresco.
Open the window so fresh air can come in.

Voy a salir a tomar aire.
I'm going to go out to get some air.

Me gusta sentir el aire en la cara.
I like feeling the air on my face.

Prende el aire.
Turn on the air conditioning.

El aire huele a lluvia.
The air smells like rain.

Todo quedó en el aire después de la junta.
Everything was left up in the air after the meeting.

El globo se fue volando por los aires.
The balloon flew away through the air.

Él se da aires de saberlo todo.
He puts on airs of knowing everything.

No te des aires de superioridad.
Don't put on airs of superiority.

89 – fuego

fire, flame

El fuego empezó en la cocina.
The fire started in the kitchen.

No te acerques tanto al fuego.
Don't get so close to the fire.

Apaga el fuego de la estufa.
Turn off the flame on the stove.

Cocina la carne a fuego lento.
Cook the meat over low heat.

El fuego nos mantuvo calientes.
The fire kept us warm.

Trae más leña para el fuego.
Bring more wood for the fire.

El fuego sigue ardiendo.
The fire is still burning.

Encendimos el fuego con papel y ramas secas.
We lit the fire with paper and dry sticks.

Los fuegos artificiales empezaron a las diez.
The fireworks started at ten.

Los fuegos artificiales iluminaron el cielo.
The fireworks lit up the sky.

90 – calor

heat

Hoy hace mucho calor.
It's really hot today.

No aguanto este calor.
I can't stand this heat.

El calor me da sueño.
The heat makes me sleepy.

Con este calor, mejor quedarnos en casa.
With this heat, we better stay home.

Hace tanto calor que no puedo dormir.
It's so hot I can't sleep.

Con este calor, sólo quiero agua fría.
With this heat, I just want cold water.

¿Prendemos el aire? Hace calor.
Should we turn on the AC? It's hot.

En el calor del momento, dije cosas que no quería.
In the heat of the moment, I said things I didn't mean.

En mayo empieza el calor.
The hot weather starts in May.

Estas olas de calor están insoportables.
These heat waves are unbearable.

91 – miedo | **fear**

91 – miedo	**fear**
Le tengo miedo a las arañas.	I'm afraid of spiders.
Mi esposo le tiene miedo a las alturas.	My husband is afraid of heights.
Él fingió ser valiente, pero tenía miedo.	He pretended to be brave, but he was afraid.
No tengas miedo, todo saldrá bien.	Don't be afraid, everything will be fine.
El miedo te mantiene a salvo.	Fear keeps you safe.
Los peores líderes usan el miedo para gobernar.	The worst leaders use fear to rule.
Todos tenemos miedos.	We all have fears.
Mis mayores miedos son la muerte y los impuestos.	My greatest fears are death and taxes.
Los miedos cambian con el tiempo.	Fears change over time.
Debemos superar nuestros miedos.	We must overcome our fears.

92 – música	**music**
Escucho música mientras estudio.	I listen to music while I study.
Me gusta escuchar música mientras manejo.	I like listening to music while driving.
Esta música me trae recuerdos.	This music brings back memories.
Escucho música de diferentes países.	I listen to music from different countries.
¿Qué tipo de música te gusta?	What kind of music do you like?
La música del restaurante está muy alta.	The restaurant's music is too loud.
Bájale a la música.	Turn down the music.
Ella estudia música en el conservatorio.	She studies music at the conservatory.
La música me pone de buen humor.	Music puts me in a good mood.
Una fiesta sin música es aburrida.	A party without music is boring.

93 – suerte	**luck**
¡Buena suerte!	Good luck!
Qué mala suerte.	What bad luck.
Te deseo suerte.	I wish you luck.
Por suerte, todo salió bien.	Luckily, everything turned out fine.
Fue pura suerte, nada más.	It was pure luck, nothing more.
No fue la suerte, fue trabajo duro.	It wasn't luck, it was hard work.
La suerte favorece a los preparados.	Luck favors the prepared.
No confíes tanto en la suerte.	Don't rely too much on luck.
Con suerte llego antes de las cinco.	With luck I'll arrive before five.
Probé mi suerte en el casino.	I tried my luck at the casino.

94 – ayuda | **help, aid**

Con un poco de ayuda, acabamos rápido. | With a bit of help, we'll finish fast.
No quiero ayuda, puedo hacerlo yo mismo. | I don't want help, I can do it myself.
Necesito tu ayuda con la tarea de matemáticas. | I need your help with the mathematics homework.
Sin tu ayuda, habría sido un desastre. | Without your help, it would've been a disaster.
La ayuda humanitaria ya está en camino. | The humanitarian aid is already on the way.
No tengo más remedio que pedir ayuda. | I have no choice but to ask for help.
Pedir ayuda no es señal de debilidad. | Asking for help isn't a sign of weakness.
Gracias por tu ayuda, de verdad la necesitaba. | Thank you for your help, I truly needed it.
Tu ayuda hizo toda la diferencia. | Your help made all the difference.
Las ayudas visuales facilitan el aprendizaje. | Visual aids make learning easier.

95 – banco | **bank, bench**

El banco está lleno de gente los lunes. | The bank is full of people on Mondays.
Necesito ir al banco antes de que cierre. | I need to go to the bank before it closes.
El banco cierra a las cuatro de la tarde. | The bank closes at four in the afternoon.
El banco no abre los domingos. | The bank doesn't open on Sundays.
Mi papá trabaja en un banco internacional. | My dad works at an international bank.
Cambié pesos en el banco de la esquina. | I exchanged pesos at the bank on the corner.
El banco me negó el préstamo. | The bank denied me the loan.
Me senté en el banco del parque a leer. | I sat on the park bench to read.
Hay bancos nuevos en la plaza. | There are new benches in the plaza.
Un artista pintó todos los bancos de este parque. | An artist painted all the benches in this park.

96 – gato | **cat**

Mi gato duerme casi todo el día. | My cat sleeps almost all day.
El gato maúlla cuando tiene hambre. | The cat meows when it's hungry.
El gato ronronea cuando come. | The cat purrs when it eats.
A mi gato no le gustan las visitas. | My cat doesn't like visitors.
El gato se escondió debajo de la cama. | The cat hid under the bed.
Cierra la puerta, que el gato no se escape. | Close the door so the cat doesn't escape.
Mi gata tuvo tres gatitos. | My cat had three kittens.
En las noches frías, mis gatos se acurrucan juntos. | On cold nights, my cats snuggle together.
Se dice que los gatos tienen nueve vidas. | It is said that cats have nine lives.
Soy alérgico a los gatos. | I'm allergic to cats.

97 – carne | **meat**

No como carne. | I don't eat meat.
¿Qué tipo de carne es? | What kind of meat is it?
La carne es mucho más cara hoy en día. | Meat is much more expensive these days.
Los viernes no como carne. | I don't eat meat on Friday.
Esa taquería tiene buena carne. | That taco stand has good meat.
La carne está muy tierna y jugosa. | The meat is very tender and juicy.
¿Qué tipo de carne prefieres? | What type of meat do you prefer?
La carne de res es mi favorita. | Beef is my favorite.
Dame medio kilo de carne molida. | Give me half a kilo of ground meat.
¿Dónde están las carnes frías? | Where are the cold cuts?

98 – médico | **doctor, physician**

¿Ya fuiste al médico? | Did you go to the doctor already?
Tengo cita con el médico. | I have an appointment with the doctor.
El médico dice que no es grave. | The doctor says it's not serious.
Llama al médico si el niño tiene fiebre alta. | Call the doctor if the child has a high fever.
Mi esposa es médica pediatra. | My wife is a pediatric doctor.
Le pregunté a la médica sobre mis síntomas. | I asked the doctor about my symptoms.
La médica me dijo que todo está bien. | The doctor told me everything is fine.
Los médicos ganan bien. | Doctors earn well.
No hay suficientes médicos en el país. | There aren't enough doctors in the country.
Hay escasez de médicos en las zonas rurales. | There is a shortage of doctors in rural areas.

99 – chico, chica | **boy, girl**

¿Quién es ese chico de camisa azul? | Who is that boy in the blue shirt?
Ese chico es nuevo en el colegio. | That boy is new at school.
Hay un chico esperando en la puerta. | There's a boy waiting at the door.
¿Eres amigo de la chica que vive al lado? | Are you friends with the girl who lives next door?
La chica de allá te está mirando. | The girl over there is looking at you.
¿Conoces a la chica del vestido negro? | Do you know the girl in the black dress?
Voy a recoger a los chicos. | I'm going to pick up the kids.
Vámonos, chicos. | Let's go, guys.
Las chicas van al cine esta noche. | The girls are going to the movies tonight.
Las chicas se fueron de viaje a Oaxaca. | The girls went on a trip to Oaxaca.

100 – cielo | **sky, heaven**

El cielo está nublado. | The sky is cloudy.
Mira el cielo. ¿Crees que va a llover? | Look at the sky. Do you think it's going to rain?
El cielo se puso gris antes de llover. | The sky turned gray before raining.
Me gusta ver las nubes en el cielo. | I enjoy watching the clouds in the sky.
¿Los perros van al cielo? | Do dogs go to heaven?
Mis padres moverían cielo y tierra por mí. | My parents would move heaven and earth for me.
¡Santo cielo, qué susto me diste! | Good heavens, you gave me such a fright!
Por el amor del cielo, cálmate. | For heaven's sake, calm down.
Los cielos estuvieron grises toda la semana. | The skies were gray all week.
En fotos de viaje, los cielos siempre se ven increíbles. | In travel photos, the skies always look incredible.

101 – perro | **dog**

Estoy buscando un perro para adoptar. | I'm looking for a dog to adopt.
Ese perro está bien entrenado. | That dog is well trained.
Mi perro se pone contento cada vez que llego a casa. | My dog gets happy every time I get home.
El perro quiere salir a pasear. | The dog wants to go out for a walk.
Tengo que sacar al perro a pasear. | I have to take the dog out for a walk.
Ojalá que ese perro dejara de ladrar. | I wish that dog would stop barking.
Los niños le tienen miedo a ese perro. | The kids are afraid of that dog.
Mi perro no se lleva bien con otros perros. | My dog doesn't get along with other dogs.
Los perros del parque siempre están jugando juntos. | The dogs at the park are always playing together.
Los perros no pueden comer chocolate. | Dogs can't eat chocolate.

102 – fruta | **fruit**

Compré fruta fresca en el mercado. | I bought fresh fruit at the market.
La fruta del mercado es más barata. | The fruit at the market is cheaper.
Prefiero la fruta natural, sin azúcar. | I prefer natural fruit, without sugar.
La fruta de temporada sabe mejor. | Seasonal fruit tastes better.
La fruta se dañó por el calor. | The fruit went bad because of the heat.
La fruta atrae moscas. | Fruit attracts flies.
Me gustan casi todas las frutas. | I like almost all fruits.
Las frutas son buenas para la salud. | Fruits are good for your health.
A los niños les gustan las frutas con yogur. | Children like fruits with yogurt.
Debes lavar bien las frutas antes de comerlas. | You should wash the fruits well before eating them.

103 – pelo

hair

Se me empezó a caer el pelo hace pocos años. I started losing my hair a few years ago.
Encontré un pelo en la sopa. I found a hair in the soup.
Ese pelo es demasiado largo para ser mío. That hair is too long to be mine.
Mi abuela tenía el pelo negro en su juventud. My grandmother had black hair in her youth.
Mamá, cepíllame el pelo. Mom, brush my hair.
Este cepillo quita el pelo de mascotas de tu ropa. This brush removes pet hair from your clothes.
Me estoy dejando crecer el pelo. I'm letting my hair grow out.
Esa historia me puso los pelos de punta. That story made my hair stand on end.
El gato dejó pelos por todo el sofá. The cat left hair all over the couch.
El perro deja pelos por toda la casa. The dog leaves hair all over the house.

104 – tarea

task, chore, homework, assignment

¿Ya hiciste la tarea? Did you already do your homework?
No he terminado mi tarea de matemáticas. I haven't finished my mathematics homework.
Tengo mucha tarea para esta noche. I have a lot of homework tonight.
La tarea del gerente es supervisar al equipo. The manager's task is to supervise the team.
Esa tarea requiere mucha paciencia. That task requires a lot of patience.
Me están esperando muchas tareas en la oficina. Many tasks are waiting for me at the office.
Las tareas de esta semana estuvieron pesadas. This week's assignments were tough.
No alcancé a hacer todas las tareas. I didn't manage to do all the assignments.
Repartimos las tareas entre todos. We divided the chores among everyone.
Las tareas domésticas nunca se acaban. Household chores never end.

105 – pareja

partner, couple

Busco una pareja para bailar. I'm looking for a partner to dance with.
¿Ya tienes pareja para el baile? Do you already have a partner for the dance?
La pareja celebró su aniversario en Cancún. The couple celebrated their anniversary in Cancun.
Mi pareja y yo vivimos juntos. My partner and I live together.
La pareja adoptó un perro. The couple adopted a dog.
Una nueva pareja se mudó al lado. A new couple moved in next door.
Ellos han sido pareja desde hace cinco años. They've been a couple for five years.
Mi tío vive en pareja pero no está casado. My uncle lives with a partner but isn't married.
Hay muchas parejas en el parque. There are many couples in the park.
Esas parejas se ven felices. Those couples look happy.

106 – estudiante
Soy estudiante de medicina.
El estudiante le pidió ayuda al profesor.
¿Eres estudiante de tiempo completo?
Solo un estudiante ganará la beca.
Mi hija es estudiante en una universidad local.
Hay muchos estudiantes extranjeros en la universidad.
¿Hay descuento para estudiantes?
Cuatro estudiantes hicieron trampa en el examen.
Conocí a mi esposa cuando ambos éramos estudiantes.
Dos estudiantes se pelearon en el recreo.

student
I'm a medical student.
The student asked the teacher for help.
Are you a full-time student?
Only one student will win the scholarship.
My daughter is a student at a local university.
There are many foreign students at the university.
Is there a discount for students?
Four students cheated on the exam.
I met my wife when we were both students.
Two students got into a fight during recess.

107 – carrera
Mi hermana terminó su carrera de medicina.
¿Ya elegiste qué carrera estudiarás?
¿Qué carrera estudias?
Estoy interesado en dos carreras.
Ya va a empezar la carrera.
La carrera estuvo muy emocionante hasta el final.
¿Tener hijos afectará mi carrera?
Mi esposo me apoya en mi carrera.
Estoy pensando en cambiar de carrera.
Las carreras de salud son exigentes.

race, career, university degree program
My sister finished her medical degree.
Have you chosen what degree you'll study?
What's your major?
I'm interested in two degree programs.
The race is about to start.
The race was very exciting until the end.
Will having children affect my career?
My husband supports me in my career.
I'm thinking about changing careers.
Health-related careers are demanding.

108 – viaje
El viaje fue corto pero divertido.
Nos vamos de viaje a Costa Rica.
El viaje salió perfectamente, sin ningún problema.
Cancelaron el viaje por el clima.
¡Que tengas un buen viaje!
Ella está en un viaje de trabajo.
Mis padres pagan los viajes familiares.
Los viajes escolares siempre me emocionaban.
No me gustan los viajes largos.
Los viajes con amigos son divertidos.

trip, journey, voyage
The trip was short but fun.
We're going on a trip to Costa Rica.
The trip went perfectly, without any problem.
They canceled the trip because of the weather.
Have a good trip!
She's on a work trip.
My parents pay for family trips.
School trips always made me excited.
I don't like long trips.
Trips with friends are fun.

109 – policía	**police, police officer**
Llama a la policía.	Call the police.
La policía no hace nada.	The police don't do anything.
Mi tío es policía.	My uncle is a police officer.
La policía llegó rápido y está investigando.	The police arrived quickly and are investigating.
El policía me paró en la intersección.	The police officer stopped me at the intersection.
El policía me dio una multa.	The police officer gave me a ticket.
Aparecieron policías en cuestión de minutos.	Police officers appeared within minutes.
Se acercaron policías para hacer preguntas.	Police officers approached to ask questions.
Había policías en cada esquina.	There were police officers on every corner.
Los policías hablaron con los vecinos.	The officers spoke with the neighbors.

110 – oficina	**office**
Trabajo en la oficina tres días por semana.	I work in the office three days per week.
También trabajo desde mi oficina en casa.	I also work from my home office.
Voy a la oficina en metro.	I go to the office by subway.
Dejé mi chaqueta en la oficina.	I left my jacket in the office.
La oficina está cerrada hoy.	The office is closed today.
¿Dónde está tu oficina?	Where is your office?
Trabajo en una oficina del centro.	I work in an office downtown.
Mi oficina tiene buena vista.	My office has a good view.
Las oficinas están en el décimo piso.	The offices are on the tenth floor.
Todas las oficinas de gobierno están cerradas hoy.	All government offices are closed today.

111 – película	**movie**
La película dura dos horas.	The movie is two hours long.
¿Ya has visto esa película?	Have you seen that movie yet?
No he visto esa película.	I haven't seen that movie.
La película estuvo buenísima.	The movie was really good.
Esa película me hizo llorar.	That movie made me cry.
La película ganó varios premios.	The movie won several awards.
Vemos películas juntos en familia.	We watch movies together as a family.
Veo muchas películas.	I watch a lot of movies.
Las películas de terror me asustan.	Horror movies scare me.
Me gustan las películas de acción.	I like action movies.

112 – zapato | **shoe**

Tengo una piedra en el zapato.	I have a rock in my shoe.
El zapato izquierdo tiene un hueco.	The left shoe has a hole.
Se me perdió un zapato.	I lost a shoe.
¿Dónde está mi otro zapato?	Where is my other shoe?
Necesito unos zapatos impermeables.	I need some waterproof shoes.
¿Cuánto cuestan estos zapatos?	How much do these shoes cost?
Los zapatos son muy pequeños para mí.	The shoes are too small for me.
Estos zapatos son buenísimos para hacer senderismo.	These shoes are great for hiking.
Los zapatos negros van con todo.	Black shoes go with everything.
¿Cuándo aprenden a amarrarse los zapatos los niños?	When do kids learn to tie their shoes?

113 – bebé | **baby**

¿Cómo se llama el bebé?	What's the baby's name?
¿Cuántos meses tiene el bebé?	How many months old is the baby?
El bebé ya tiene tres meses.	The baby is already three months old.
El bebé se parece a su papá.	The baby looks like his dad.
Qué bebé tan lindo.	What a beautiful baby.
¿El bebé ya comió?	Did the baby already eat?
Dejaron al bebé con los abuelos.	They left the baby with the grandparents.
Todos los bebés lloran cuando tienen hambre.	All babies cry when they're hungry.
Los bebés necesitan dormir mucho.	Babies need to sleep a lot.
Los bebés duermen casi todo el día.	Babies sleep almost all day.

114 – maestro | **teacher**

El maestro no solo enseña, también inspira.	The teacher doesn't just teach, he also inspires.
El maestro nos pidió silencio.	The teacher asked us to be quiet.
La maestra me ayudó cuando más lo necesitaba.	The teacher helped me when I needed it most.
¿Qué dice la maestra?	What does the teacher say?
Mi maestra favorita es la señora Sánchez.	My favorite teacher is Mrs. Sanchez.
Los maestros deberían ganar más dinero.	Teachers should get paid more money.
Los maestros de mi escuela son estrictos.	The teachers at my school are strict.
Mis maestras siempre tenían paciencia conmigo.	My teachers were always patient with me.
Mis maestras hacían que aprender fuera divertido.	My teachers made learning fun.
Las maestras hablaron con todos los padres.	The teachers talked with all the parents.

115 – computadora | **computer**

Uso la computadora todos los días. | I use the computer every day.
No puedo trabajar sin computadora. | I can't work without a computer.
Trabajo en la computadora ocho horas diarias. | I work on the computer eight hours daily.
Apago mi computadora todas las noches. | I turn off my computer every night.
Mi computadora es muy lenta. | My computer is very slow.
Compré una computadora nueva ayer. | I bought a new computer yesterday.
¿Dónde compraste tu computadora? | Where did you buy your computer?
Les regalé mi vieja computadora a mis papás. | I gave my old computer to my parents.
Las computadoras del colegio son viejas. | The school computers are old.
¿Cuántas computadoras hay en el laboratorio? | How many computers are there in the lab?

116 – parque | **park**

Vamos al parque. | Let's go to the park.
El parque está lleno de niños jugando. | The park is full of children playing.
Vamos a dar un paseo por el parque. | Let's take a walk through the park.
Plantaron árboles nuevos en el parque. | They planted new trees in the park.
Ese parque tiene una gran vista de la ciudad. | That park has a great view of the city.
Mi abuelo jugaba béisbol en ese parque. | My grandfather used to play baseball in that park.
¿Conoces los parques de esta zona? | Do you know the parks in this area?
Hay muchos parques en este barrio. | There are many parks in this neighborhood.
Cuidan bien los parques aquí. | They take good care of the parks here.
Los parques más antiguos tienen árboles más grandes. | Older parks have bigger trees.

117 – equipo | **team, equipment**

Mi equipo ganó el partido. | My team won the game.
El equipo local tiene ventaja. | The home team has an advantage.
El equipo de fútbol entrena cinco días a la semana. | The soccer team trains five days per week.
El equipo tiene un nuevo entrenador este año. | The team has a new coach this year.
Compré equipo de buceo para las vacaciones. | I bought diving equipment for vacation.
Una ambulancia lleva mucho equipo médico. | An ambulance carries a lot of medical equipment.
Heredé el equipo de pesca de mi abuelo. | I inherited my grandfather's fishing equipment.
Todos los equipos quieren fichar a ese jugador. | All the teams want to sign that player.
Los equipos se están preparando para el torneo. | The teams are preparing for the tournament.
¿Cuántos equipos hay en el torneo? | How many teams are in the tournament?

118 – juego

game

Este juego es muy divertido.
This game is really fun.

Me encanta el juego de mesa nuevo.
I love the new board game.

Perdí el juego por un punto.
I lost the game by one point.

El juego terminó en empate.
The game ended in a tie.

El juego fue más difícil de lo que pensé.
The game was harder than I thought.

El juego duró más de dos horas.
The game lasted more than two hours.

Instalé varios juegos en mi teléfono.
I installed several games on my phone.

Me gusta ver los Juegos Olímpicos.
I like to watch the Olympic Games.

Los juegos de mesa son mi pasatiempo.
Board games are my hobby.

Mis hijos aman los juegos de video.
My kids love video games.

119 – plato

plate

El plato está caliente, ten cuidado.
The plate is hot, be careful.

Pon tu plato sucio en el fregadero.
Put your dirty plate in the sink.

¿Cuál es el plato del día?
What is the daily special?

Necesito cambiar este plato roto.
I need to replace this broken plate.

¿Qué platos vamos a utilizar para la cena de Navidad?
Which plates are we using for Christmas dinner?

Hay que lavar los platos después de cenar.
We have to wash the dishes after dinner.

Me toca lavar los platos hoy.
It's my turn to do the dishes today.

¿Puedes secar los platos?
Can you dry the dishes?

Usamos los platos grandes para la cena.
We use the big plates for dinner.

Los platos se rompieron en la mudanza.
The plates broke during the move.

120 – ventana

window

Abre la ventana, por favor.
Open the window, please.

Me gusta sentarme junto a la ventana.
I like sitting next to the window.

La pelota rompió la ventana.
The ball broke the window.

Cierra la ventana, hace frío.
Close the window, it's cold.

No dejes pasar esa ventana de oportunidad.
Don't let that window of opportunity pass.

Mi gato se pasa todo el día viendo por la ventana.
My cat spends all day looking out the window.

Las ventanas viejas no cierran bien.
The old windows don't close properly.

Dentro de poco, vamos a instalar las ventanas nuevas.
Soon, we're going to install the new windows.

Están limpiando las ventanas del edificio.
They're cleaning the building's windows.

Cerraron las ventanas por la lluvia.
They closed the windows because of the rain.

121 – curso — **course, class**

Me inscribí a un curso en línea.	I signed up for an online course.
El curso cuesta mil pesos.	The course costs a thousand pesos.
Aprendimos mucho durante el curso.	We learned a lot during the course.
Terminé el curso con buenas calificaciones.	I finished the course with good grades.
Voy a tomar un curso de cocina italiana.	I'm going to take an Italian cooking course.
El curso se imparte los martes.	The course is taught on Tuesdays.
Me faltan dos cursos para graduarme.	I'm missing two courses to graduate.
Los cursos de idiomas son populares.	Language courses are popular.
Los cursos nocturnos me sirven más.	Evening courses work better for me.
Algunos cursos son presenciales, otros en línea.	Some courses are in person, others online.

122 – zona — **area, zone, region**

Esta zona de la ciudad es muy segura.	This area of the city is very safe.
Es una zona segura para caminar.	It's a safe area to walk.
Esa zona es peligrosa de noche.	That area is dangerous at night.
No conozco bien esa zona.	I don't know that area well.
¿De qué zona de la ciudad eres?	What area of the city are you from?
Es una zona donde hay muchos árboles.	It's an area where there are lots of trees.
Esta zona tiene muchos restaurantes.	This area has lots of restaurants.
Estas zonas se pusieron muy de moda.	These areas became very trendy.
Las zonas turísticas están llenas en verano.	Tourist areas are crowded in summer.
Las zonas escolares tienen límite de velocidad.	School zones have a speed limit.

123 – pollo — **chicken**

Hoy comemos arroz con pollo.	Today we're eating rice with chicken.
¿Quieres pollo asado para la cena?	Do you want roasted chicken for dinner?
Me encanta el pollo a la parrilla.	I love grilled chicken.
Voy a comprar un pollo entero en el mercado.	I'm going to buy a whole chicken at the market.
Los tacos de pollo en esta taquería son buenísimos.	The chicken tacos at this taco place are really good.
Se me antoja sopa de pollo.	I'm craving chicken soup.
Como pollo, pero no carne roja.	I eat chicken but not red meat.
Sabe a pollo.	Tastes like chicken.
El pollo tiende a estar mucho más seco al día siguiente.	Chicken tends to be much drier the next day.
Vamos a cocinar dos pollos para la reunión.	We're going to cook two chickens for the gathering.

124 – piso	**floor**
Cuidado, el piso está mojado.	Careful, the floor is wet.
El edificio tiene diez pisos.	The building has ten floors.
¿En qué piso vives?	What floor do you live on?
Vivo en el cuarto piso.	I live on the fourth floor.
Mis papás viven un piso arriba de nosotros.	My parents live one floor above us.
Los últimos pisos tienen vista a la ciudad.	The top floors have a view of the city.
Los primeros dos pisos son oficinas.	The first two floors are offices.
Los pisos viejos crujen cuando caminas.	Old floors creak when you walk.
Cambiaron los pisos de toda la casa.	They replaced the floors in the whole house.
Me gusta cómo quedaron los pisos nuevos.	I like how the new floors turned out.

125 – respuesta	**answer, response, reply**
Necesito una respuesta antes del viernes.	I need an answer before Friday.
Aún estoy esperando su respuesta.	I'm still waiting for their reply.
Esa no era la respuesta que estaba esperando.	That wasn't the answer I was expecting.
Gracias por tu rápida respuesta.	Thanks for your quick reply.
La respuesta correcta está al final del libro.	The correct answer is at the end of the book.
No mires la respuesta antes de intentar resolverlo.	Don't look at the answer before trying to solve it.
La respuesta fue un rotundo "no".	The answer was a firm "no."
Las respuestas muestran que entendiste el tema.	The answers show that you understood the topic.
No entiendo algunas de tus respuestas.	I don't understand some of your answers.
Necesito respuestas, no más excusas.	I need answers, not more excuses.

126 – pie	**foot**
Vamos a pie, está muy cerca.	Let's go on foot, it's really close.
Se me durmió el pie.	My foot fell asleep.
No puedo correr porque me duele mucho el pie.	I can't run because my foot hurts too much.
Tengo una fractura en el pie izquierdo.	I have a fracture in my left foot.
Me torcí el pie jugando fútbol.	I twisted my foot playing soccer.
Tengo una ampolla en el pie por los zapatos nuevos.	I have a blister on my foot from the new shoes.
Siento un calambre en el pie que no se me quita.	I feel a cramp in my foot that won't go away.
No apoyes los pies en la mesa.	Don't put your feet on the table.
Estos zapatos no me calientan los pies en invierno.	These shoes don't keep my feet warm in winter.
Caminar descalzo es bueno para tus pies.	Walking barefoot is good for your feet.

127 – fin — **end, conclusion, purpose, goal**

Ese fue el fin de su carrera. — That was the end of his career.
Voy a poner fin a la discusión. — I'm going to put an end to this discussion.
¡Por fin es viernes! — It's finally Friday!
El fin no justifica los medios. — The end doesn't justify the means.
Todo llega a su fin tarde o temprano. — Everything comes to an end sooner or later.
Al fin y al cabo, ella tenía razón. — After all, she was right.
El nuevo puente tiene como fin ahorrar tiempo. — The new bridge is intended to save time.
¿Qué haces los fines de semana? — What do you do on weekends?
Los fines de semana duermo hasta tarde. — On weekends I sleep late.
Trabajo entre semana, no los fines de semana. — I work during the week, not on weekends.

128 – sentido — **sense, meaning, direction**

Lo que dices no tiene sentido. — What you're saying doesn't make sense.
Él tiene un gran sentido del humor. — He has a great sense of humor.
En ese sentido, estoy de acuerdo contigo. — In that sense, I agree with you.
Los perros tienen un gran sentido del olfato. — Dogs have a great sense of smell.
Tengo buen sentido de la orientación. — I have a good sense of direction.
¿Cuál es el sentido de la vida? — What is the meaning of life?
Usa todos tus sentidos para disfrutar la comida. — Use all your senses to enjoy the food.
Los sentidos se agudizan cuando tienes miedo. — Your senses sharpen when you're afraid.
La naturaleza despierta mis sentidos. — Nature awakens my senses.
Bloquearon la calle en ambos sentidos. — They blocked the street in both directions.

129 – reunión — **meeting, gathering**

Pablo tiene una reunión con su jefe hoy al mediodía. — Pablo has a meeting with his boss today at noon.
La reunión fue bastante productiva. — The meeting was pretty productive.
Evito programar reuniones después de las cinco. — I avoid scheduling meetings after five.
La reunión empezó sin mí. — The meeting started without me.
Hoy tengo seis reuniones. — I have six meetings today.
Me paso todo el día en reuniones. — I spend all day in meetings.
Las reuniones de equipo son los lunes. — Team meetings are on Mondays.
Odio las reuniones que pudieron haber sido un correo. — I hate meetings that could have been an email.
Trato de hacer reuniones cortas. — I try to make meetings short.
La Navidad es un tiempo para reuniones familiares. — Christmas is a time for family gatherings

130 – futuro | **future**

Pienso mucho en el futuro. | I think a lot about the future.
Me preocupa mi futuro. | I'm worried about my future.
El futuro es incierto. | The future is uncertain.
Nadie sabe qué traerá el futuro. | No one knows what the future will bring.
No pienses tanto en el futuro. | Don't think so much about the future.
El futuro del país está en nuestras manos. | The country's future is in our hands.
Hay que construir un mejor futuro. | We have to build a better future.
No te preocupes por el futuro. | Don't worry about the future.
¿Qué te depara el futuro? | What does the future hold for you?
En el futuro me gustaría viajar más. | In the future I'd like to travel more.

131 – voz | **voice**

Me gusta la voz de ese cantante. | I like that singer's voice.
No levantes la voz, por favor. | Don't raise your voice, please.
Esa voz me suena familiar. | That voice sounds familiar to me.
Reconocí su voz instantáneamente. | I recognized his voice instantly.
Mi hijo de dos años tiene una voz adorable. | My two-year-old son has an adorable voice.
Se me fue la voz por gritar tanto. | I lost my voice from shouting so much.
Él lo dijo en voz alta para todos. | He said it out loud for everyone.
Oigo voces en el pasillo. | I hear voices in the hallway.
Oigo voces, pero no veo a nadie. | I hear voices, but I don't see anyone.
Las voces de los niños llenan la casa. | The children's voices fill the house.

132 – salud | **health**

Fumar daña tu salud. | Smoking damages your health.
Hacer ejercicio es bueno para la salud. | Exercising is good for your health.
La buena alimentación es clave para la salud. | Good nutrition is key to health.
Cambié mi dieta por razones de salud. | I changed my diet for health reasons.
Es importante cuidar la salud mental. | It's important to take care of mental health.
Ella siempre se preocupa por la salud de su familia. | She always worries about her family's health.
La salud de los niños es una prioridad. | Children's health is a priority.
Perdimos nuestra casa, pero aún tenemos salud. | We lost our house, but we still have our health.
Levantaron las copas y gritaron "¡Salud!". | They raised their glasses and shouted "Cheers!"
¡Salud! le dije cuando estornudó en la oficina. | Bless you! I said when he sneezed in the office.

133 – profesor — **teacher, professor**

El profesor canceló la clase de hoy. — The professor canceled today's class.
¿A qué hora tiene horario de oficina el profesor? — What time does the professor have office hours?
Profesor, ¿podría explicar este concepto otra vez? — Professor, could you explain this concept again?
Mi profesor de cálculo es muy exigente. — My calculus professor is really demanding.
La profesora contesta los correos muy rápido. — The professor answers emails very quickly.
La profesora Martínez tiene un doctorado en física. — Professor Martínez has a doctorate in physics.
Mi hermana es profesora en la universidad. — My sister is a professor at the university.
La profesora de química explicó el experimento. — The chemistry professor explained the experiment.
¿Los profesores de tu facultad publican mucho? — Do the professors in your faculty publish a lot?
Los profesores de la facultad se reúnen cada mes. — The faculty professors meet every month.

134 – fuerza — **strength, force, power**

Usa toda tu fuerza. — Use all your strength.
No tengo fuerza para levantar esta caja. — I don't have the strength to lift this box.
No tengo la fuerza para seguir discutiendo. — I don't have the strength to keep arguing.
Usa la técnica, no solo la fuerza. — Use technique, not just strength.
La fuerza del viento tumbó varios árboles. — The force of the wind knocked down several trees.
Mi familia y mi religión me dan fuerza. — My family and religion give me strength.
La fuerza de voluntad es importante. — Willpower is important.
Unieron fuerzas para lograrlo. — They joined forces to achieve it.
Hazlo con todas tus fuerzas. — Do it with all your strength.
Ya no tengo fuerzas. — I don't have any strength left.

135 – cuarto — **room, bedroom**

Mi cuarto está en el segundo piso. — My room is on the second floor.
El cuarto de los niños siempre está desordenado. — The children's room is always messy.
Rentamos un cuarto por una noche. — We rented a room for one night.
No entres a mi cuarto sin tocar. — Don't come into my room without knocking.
Ese cuarto no tiene ventanas. — That room has no windows.
El cuarto de mi hermano huele muy mal. — My brother's room smells really bad.
Solo quiero llegar a mi cuarto y dormir. — I just want to get to my room and sleep.
Los cuartos de arriba son más cálidos. — The upstairs rooms are warmer.
Vamos a repintar los cuartos de arriba. — We are going to repaint the rooms upstairs.
Pintaron todos los cuartos de blanco. — They painted all the rooms white.

136 – barrio	**neighborhood**
¿En qué barrio vives?	What neighborhood do you live in?
Somos del mismo barrio.	We're from the same neighborhood.
Mi barrio es muy tranquilo y seguro.	My neighborhood is very quiet and safe.
En mi barrio hay tiendas por todos lados.	In my neighborhood there are shops everywhere.
Mi barrio está cerca del metro.	My neighborhood is close to the subway.
El barrio ha cambiado mucho desde que me fui.	The neighborhood has changed a lot since I left.
Cada barrio tiene su propio estilo.	Each neighborhood has its own style.
En esta ciudad hay muchos barrios distintos.	There are many different neighborhoods in this city.
Hay barrios a los que no debes entrar.	There are neighborhoods you shouldn't go into.
Algunos barrios ya están gentrificados.	Some neighborhoods are already gentrified.

137 – noticia	**news**
Recibí una noticia inesperada.	I got an unexpected piece of news.
Me enteré de una noticia muy triste.	I found out about a very sad piece of news.
Esa noticia cambió mis planes.	That news changed my plans.
La noticia del accidente fue confirmada.	The news of the accident was confirmed.
¿Tienes noticias de tu hermano?	Do you have news from your brother?
No tengo noticias de él.	I have no news from him.
Mi abuelo ve las noticias todas las noches.	My grandpa watches the news every night.
Leo demasiado las noticias.	I read the news too much.
Las noticias de hoy fueron horribles.	Today's news was horrible.
Hay muchas noticias malas últimamente.	There's a lot of bad news lately.

138 – lluvia	**rain**
Me gusta el sonido de la lluvia.	I like the sound of rain.
La lluvia cayó toda la noche.	The rain fell all night.
Hay pronóstico de lluvia.	There's rain in the forecast.
La lluvia arruinó nuestros planes.	The rain ruined our plans.
No esperaba tanta lluvia hoy.	I didn't expect so much rain today.
Se suspendió el partido por la lluvia.	The game was suspended due to rain.
Después de la lluvia, salió el sol.	After the rain, the sun came out.
Necesitamos la lluvia para las cosechas.	We need the rain for the crops.
¿Alguna vez has visto una lluvia de meteoros?	Have you ever seen a meteor shower?
La temporada de lluvias inicia en mayo.	The rainy season begins in May.

139 – jefe, jefa — **boss**

Mi jefe me dio el día libre. — My boss gave me the day off.
El jefe llega temprano a la oficina. — The boss arrives early at the office.
El jefe pasa el día apagando incendios. — The boss spends the day putting out fires.
Tengo que pedirle permiso a mi jefe. — I have to ask my boss for permission.
Mi jefa me aumentó el sueldo. — My boss gave me a raise.
Necesito hablar con la jefa ahora. — I need to speak with the boss now.
La jefa está de buen humor hoy. — The boss is in a good mood today.
Mi jefa es muy exigente pero justa. — My boss is very demanding but fair.
Los jefes están reunidos en la sala de juntas. — The bosses are meeting in the boardroom.
Los jefes decidieron dar un bono navideño. — The bosses decided to give a Christmas bonus.

140 – boca — **mouth**

Cúbrete la boca al toser. — Cover your mouth when you cough.
Cierra la boca cuando mastiques. — Close your mouth when you chew.
No hables con la boca llena. — Don't talk with your mouth full.
Límpiate la boca con la servilleta. — Wipe your mouth with your napkin.
Respira por la nariz, no por la boca. — Breathe through your nose, not your mouth.
El olor me hace agua la boca. — The smell makes my mouth water.
No pongas palabras en mi boca. — Don't put words in my mouth.
Acuéstate boca arriba. — Lie down face up.
Acuéstate boca abajo. — Lie down face down.
Tenemos muchas bocas que alimentar. — We have many mouths to feed.

141 – árbol — **tree**

Mis abuelos plantaron este árbol. — My grandparents planted this tree.
El pájaro hizo su nido en ese árbol. — The bird made its nest in that tree.
Un árbol se cayó durante la tormenta de anoche. — A tree fell during last night's storm.
Mi árbol genealógico es extenso. — My family tree is extensive.
El árbol de Navidad ya está decorado. — The Christmas tree is already decorated.
Estamos relajándonos a la sombra de un árbol. — We're relaxing under the shade of a tree.
Los árboles del parque dan mucha sombra. — The tree in the park gives a lot of shade.
Plantaron muchos árboles nuevos en la calle. — They planted many new trees on the street.
Hay árboles frutales en el huerto. — There are fruit trees in the orchard.
Me encantaba trepar a los árboles cuando era niño. — I loved climbing trees when I was young.

142 – hecho	**fact**
De hecho, tienes razón.	In fact, you're right.
No puedo negar el hecho.	I can't deny the fact.
Es un hecho comprobado.	It's a proven fact.
De hecho, me gusta mucho.	Actually, I really like it.
El hecho es que no tengo dinero.	The fact is that I don't have money.
Ese hecho lo cambia todo.	That fact changes everything.
El hecho es que no vino.	The fact is that he didn't come.
De hecho, ya lo sabía.	Actually, I already knew that.
Los hechos hablan por sí mismos.	The facts speak for themselves.
Los hechos me dan razón.	The facts prove me right.

143 – brazo	**arm**
¿Te lastimaste el brazo?	Did you hurt your arm?
Me duele el brazo.	My arm hurts.
No puedo mover el brazo.	I can't move my arm.
Él se rompió el brazo jugando fútbol.	He broke his arm playing soccer.
Mi hijo se hizo un tatuaje en el brazo izquierdo.	My son got a tattoo on his left arm.
Suéltame el brazo por favor.	Please let go of my arm.
Me pusieron la vacuna en el brazo.	They gave me the vaccine in the arm.
Lo recibieron con los brazos abiertos.	They welcomed him with open arms.
Ella lleva al bebé en los brazos.	She's carrying the baby in her arms.
Los brazos le temblaban del esfuerzo.	His arms were shaking from effort.

144 – bolsa	**bag, purse**
¿Tienes bolsa?	Do you have a bag?
No necesito bolsa.	I don't need a bag.
Pon eso en la bolsa.	Put that in the bag.
Pon todo en la bolsa.	Put everything in the bag.
¿Dónde está mi bolsa?	Where is my purse?
Creo que dejaste tu bolsa en el carro.	I think you left your purse in the car.
Ayúdame con las bolsas.	Help me with the bags.
Las bolsas están pesadas.	The bags are heavy.
Las bolsas están en el carro.	The bags are in the car.
Pon las bolsas en la mesa.	Put the bags on the table.

145 – cena | **dinner**

La cena se sirve a las ocho. | Dinner is served at eight.
La cena está lista. | Dinner is ready.
La cena estuvo deliciosa. | Dinner was delicious.
Compré ingredientes para la cena. | I bought ingredients for dinner.
No quiero una cena pesada hoy. | I don't want a heavy dinner today.
Después de la cena lavamos los platos. | After dinner we wash the dishes.
Las cenas en España siempre terminan tarde. | Dinners in Spain always end late.
Las cenas ligeras son más saludables. | Light dinners are healthier.
Organizamos cenas con amigos. | We organize dinners with friends.
Las cenas familiares son importantes. | Family dinners are important.

146 – pared | **wall**

Colgué el cuadro en la pared. | I hung the picture on the wall.
Voy a montar el nuevo televisor en la pared. | I'm going to mount the new TV on the wall.
Empuja la cama contra la pared. | Push the bed against the wall.
¿Por qué hay un agujero en la pared? ¿Qué pasó? | Why is there a hole in the wall? What happened?
Tenemos un piano de pared en casa. | We have an upright piano at home.
Las paredes necesitan otra capa de pintura. | The walls need another coat of paint.
Pintamos todas las paredes de blanco. | We painted all the walls white.
Decoré las paredes con fotos familiares. | I decorated the walls with family photos.
Escucho todo a través de estas paredes tan delgadas. | I hear everything through these thin walls.
Las paredes tienen oídos. | The walls have ears.

147 – canción | **song**

¿Cómo se llama esta canción? | What's the name of this song?
Esta canción es muy pegadiza. | This song is very catchy.
Esa canción se me quedó en la cabeza. | That song got stuck in my head.
No saco esa canción de mi mente. | I can't get that song out of my mind.
Esa canción me trae recuerdos. | That song brings back memories.
Esta era mi canción favorita cuando era niño. | This was my favorite song when I was a kid.
Me gustan más sus canciones antiguas que las nuevas. | I like her older songs better than the new ones.
Tocaron mis canciones favoritas en el concierto. | They played my favorite songs at the concert.
Me sé la letra de todas sus canciones. | I know the lyrics to all of his songs.
Sus canciones hablan de amor. | His songs talk about love.

148 – playa	**beach**
Dejé mis sandalias en la playa.	I left my sandals on the beach.
Vamos a la playa temprano para evitar el sol fuerte.	We're going to the beach early to avoid the strong sun.
Me encanta caminar por la playa al atardecer.	I love walking along the beach at sunset.
Las gaviotas te molestan si comes en la playa.	Seagulls bother you if you eat at the beach.
¿Conoces alguna playa donde no haya tanta gente?	Do you know a beach where there aren't so many people?
Los niños pasaron todo el día jugando en la playa.	The kids spent the whole day playing at the beach.
Vivir cerca de la playa es un sueño para muchos.	Living near the beach is a dream for many.
Solo me gustan las playas con agua cálida.	I only like beaches with warm water.
Prefiero las playas del Caribe porque el agua es más clara.	I prefer Caribbean beaches because the water is clearer.
Las playas de Cancún son las más visitadas por turistas.	Cancún's beaches are the most visited by tourists.

149 – silla	**chair**
Dejé mi chaqueta sobre la silla.	I left my jacket on the chair.
Esa silla está rota.	That chair is broken.
Oye, ¿me guardas la silla?	Hey, can you save my seat?
Esa silla se ve muy cómoda.	That chair looks really comfortable.
Compré una silla nueva para mi escritorio.	I bought a new chair for my desk.
Se rompió una pata de la silla y casi me caigo.	One of the chair legs broke and I almost fell.
No hay suficientes sillas para todos.	There aren't enough chairs for everyone.
Necesitamos más sillas para los invitados.	We need more chairs for the guests.
¿Cuántas sillas necesitamos?	How many chairs do we need?
Las sillas nuevas combinan con la mesa.	The new chairs match the table.

150 – colegio	**school (private)**
Ese colegio es solo para niñas.	That school is only for girls.
¿A qué hora sales del colegio?	What time do you get out of school?
Hoy hay actividades en el colegio.	Today there are activities at school.
Mis hijos estudian en un colegio bilingüe.	My children study at a bilingual school.
El colegio es caro pero tiene buena reputación.	The school is expensive but has a good reputation.
Están evaluando varios colegios.	They're evaluating several schools.
Los colegios bilingües cuestan más.	Bilingual schools cost more.
Los mejores colegios no siempre son los más caros.	The best schools aren't always the most expensive.
Algunos colegios parecen más parques que colegios.	Some schools look more like parks than schools.
Todos los colegios piden uniforme.	All schools require a uniform.

151 – nivel | **level**

Tu nivel de español ha mejorado mucho este año. | Your Spanish level has improved a lot this year.
El nivel del agua del lago está muy bajo. | The lake's water level is very low.
Hay estacionamiento en el quinto nivel. | There's parking on the fifth level.
Ese jugador está en otro nivel. | That player is on another level.
Mi nivel de estrés está por las nubes últimamente. | My stress level is through the roof lately.
A nivel personal, creo que fue una buena decisión. | On a personal level, I think it was a good decision.
Ese nivel ya me lo pasé. | I already passed that level.
Los niveles del juego están difíciles. | The game levels are tough.
Estos niveles no son para principiantes. | These levels aren't for beginners.
Alcanzamos niveles récord de ventas este trimestre. | We reached record sales levels this quarter.

152 – abuelo, abuela | **grandfather, grandmother**

Extraño mucho a mi abuelo. | I miss my grandfather a lot.
¿Cómo está tu abuelo? | How is your grandfather?
Mi abuelo cumple ochenta años mañana. | My grandfather turns eighty tomorrow.
Mi abuela da los mejores abrazos. | My grandmother gives the best hugs.
¿Has hablado con tu abuela últimamente? | Have you talked to your grandmother lately?
Mi abuela hace las mejores enchiladas. | My grandmother makes the best enchiladas.
Mis dos abuelos todavía están vivos. | Both of my grandfathers are still alive.
Mis abuelos están sanos y viajan mucho. | My grandparents are healthy and travel a lot.
Mis abuelas me regalan dulces cuando las visito. | My grandmothers give me candy when I visit them.
Mis abuelas nacieron en el mismo pueblo. | My grandmothers were born in the same town.

153 – camisa | **shirt**

Ponte esta camisa para la cena de esta noche. | Wear this shirt to dinner tonight.
Esa camisa te queda bien. | That shirt looks good on you.
Perdí un botón de la camisa. | I lost a button from the shirt.
Compré una camisa para la fiesta. | I bought a shirt for the party.
Esa camisa no combina con tu pantalón. | That shirt doesn't match your pants.
Tu camisa está arrugada. | Your shirt is wrinkled.
Todas mis camisas necesitan plancharse. | All my shirts need to be ironed.
Tengo muchas camisas blancas. | I have many white shirts.
Las camisas blancas siempre están de moda. | White shirts are always in style.
Mis camisas buenas están colgadas en el armario. | My nice shirts are hanging in the closet.

154 – arroz
Prefiero arroz en lugar de pasta.
Ese arroz tiene un olor muy rico.
Lavo el arroz antes de cocinarlo.
El arroz integral tarda más en cocinarse.
El arroz integral tiene más fibra.
El arroz se pegó en la olla.
Sobró mucho arroz de la comida.
El arroz combina con casi todo.
Mi abuela hace el mejor arroz con leche.
El arroz a la mexicana lleva jitomate y chícharos.

rice
I prefer rice instead of pasta.
That rice has a really great smell.
I wash the rice before cooking it.
Brown rice takes longer to cook.
Brown rice has more fiber.
The rice stuck to the pot.
A lot of rice was left over from the meal.
Rice goes well with almost everything.
My grandmother makes the best rice pudding.
Mexican-style rice has red tomato and peas.

155 – reloj
¿Qué tipo de reloj tienes?
Tengo un reloj inteligente que se conecta a mi celular.
Este reloj es muy bonito pero súper caro.
Mi reloj es analógico, no digital.
Se me olvidó el reloj en casa.
Se me cayó el reloj y se rayó.
No confíes en ese reloj, se atrasa.
Ese reloj antiguo fue de mi abuelo.
Mi papá colecciona relojes antiguos.
Tengo varios relojes pero casi nunca los uso.

watch, clock
What type of watch do you have?
I have a smartwatch that connects to my phone.
This watch is very pretty but super expensive.
My watch is analog, not digital.
I forgot my watch at home.
I dropped my watch and it got scratched.
Don't trust that clock, it runs slow.
That antique clock was my grandfather's.
My dad collects antique clocks.
I have several watches but I almost never use them.

156 – deporte
El fútbol es el deporte más popular en México.
¿Qué deporte te gusta más?
Mi deporte favorito es el baloncesto.
El deporte ayuda a mantenerte en forma.
El deporte olímpico más antiguo es el atletismo.
El paracaidismo es un deporte extremo.
En el colegio enseñan diferentes deportes.
Hay deportes para todas las edades.
Los deportes de invierno son caros.
La sección de deportes está en la página diez.

sport
Soccer is the most popular sport in Mexico.
What sport do you like most?
My favorite sport is basketball.
Sport helps you stay in shape.
The oldest Olympic sport is track and field.
Skydiving is an extreme sport.
At school they teach different sports.
There are sports for all ages.
Winter sports are expensive.
The sports section is on page ten.

157 – cumpleaños

birthday

Hoy es mi cumpleaños.
Today is my birthday.

¡Feliz cumpleaños!
Happy birthday!

¿Qué quieres para tu cumpleaños?
What do you want for your birthday?

No necesito ningún regalo de cumpleaños.
I don't need any birthday gifts.

Voy a celebrar mi cumpleaños con mi familia.
I'm going to celebrate my birthday with my family.

¿Cuándo es tu cumpleaños?
When is your birthday?

Mi cumpleaños es en julio.
My birthday is in July.

No olvides llamar a tu mamá por su cumpleaños.
Don't forget to call your mom on her birthday.

Le compré un pastel a ella por su cumpleaños.
I bought her a cake for her birthday.

Yo sé los cumpleaños de todos mis amigos.
I know all of my friends' birthdays.

158 – descanso

rest, break

El descanso es importante para la salud.
Rest is important for your health.

Necesitas un descanso o te vas a enfermar.
You need a rest or you're going to get sick.

No hay descanso para los padres de gemelos.
There's no rest for parents of twins.

Merecemos un descanso después de todo esto.
We deserve a break after all this.

Él pidió un descanso de cinco minutos.
He asked for a five-minute break.

Tomo un descanso cada hora.
I take a break every hour.

¿Cuánto duran los descansos?
How long are the breaks?

Mis descansos duran unos cinco minutos.
My breaks last about five minutes.

Los descansos ayudan a rendir mejor.
Breaks help you perform better.

Mis descansos en el trabajo son de quince minutos.
My breaks at work are fifteen minutes long.

159 – causa

cause

La causa del dolor aún es desconocida.
The cause of the pain is still unknown.

No entiendo la causa del problema.
I don't understand the cause of the problem.

¿Cuál fue la causa del accidente?
What was the cause of the accident?

Apoyé la causa porque me importó.
I supported the cause because I cared.

Lo hice por una buena causa.
I did it for a good cause.

Las causas no están claras.
The causes aren't clear.

No saben las causas de la falla.
They don't know the causes of the failure.

La causa del incendio sigue en estudio.
The cause of the fire is still under review.

Hay muchas causas posibles.
There are many possible causes.

Hay dos causas principales del conflicto.
There are two main causes of the conflict.

160 – sueño | **dream, sleep**

Tuve un sueño muy raro anoche. | I had a really weird dream last night.
Desde niña, mi sueño era ser doctora. | Since I was a girl, my dream was to be a doctor.
Ese sueño se sintió muy real. | That dream felt so real.
Mi sueño es viajar por el mundo. | My dream is to travel around the world.
Tengo mucho sueño. | I'm really sleepy.
Me dio sueño después de comer. | I got sleepy after eating.
Nunca dejes de perseguir tus sueños. | Never stop chasing your dreams.
Me gustan los sueños donde puedo volar. | I like dreams where I can fly.
Casi nunca recuerdo mis sueños. | I hardly ever remember my dreams.
Los sueños a veces parecen muy reales. | Dreams sometimes seem so real.

161 – huevo | **egg**

¿Quieres un huevo para desayunar? | Do you want an egg for breakfast?
¿Te gusta el huevo revuelto o frito? | Do you like your egg scrambled or fried?
Necesito un huevo para la receta del pastel. | I need an egg for the cake recipe.
Ya no hay huevos. | There are no more eggs.
Ve a la tienda y compra huevos. | Go to the store and buy some eggs.
Los huevos se venden por docena. | Eggs are sold by the dozen.
Los huevos cuestan más que antes. | Eggs cost more than before.
Los huevos son una buena fuente de proteína. | Eggs are a good source of protein.
Me encantan los huevos revueltos con jamón. | I love scrambled eggs with ham.
Los huevos estaban fríos cuando los sirvieron. | The eggs were cold when they served them.

162 – llamada | **call, phone call**

Estoy esperando una llamada importante. | I'm waiting for an important call.
Él ignoró mi llamada. | He ignored my call.
Perdí tu llamada porque estaba manejando. | I missed your call because I was driving.
¿Vas a contestar la llamada? | Are you going to answer the call?
La llamada llegó en el peor momento. | The call came at the worst moment.
No debí contestar esa llamada. | I shouldn't have answered that call.
Una llamada bastó para arreglar todo. | One call was enough to fix everything.
¿Cómo es que hoy me perdí tantas llamadas? | How did I miss so many calls today?
No contesto llamadas de números desconocidos. | I don't answer calls from unknown numbers.
Las llamadas de larga distancia ya no cuestan tanto. | Long-distance calls don't cost as much anymore.

163 – vecino | **neighbor**

¿Conoces al vecino nuevo? — Do you know the new neighbor?
Mi vecino tiene un perro amigable. — My neighbor has a friendly dog.
Escuché que mi vecino se va a mudar pronto. — I heard that my neighbor is going to move soon.
Mi vecino siempre saluda cuando pasa. — My neighbor always says hello when he walks by.
La vecina siempre sabe las noticias del barrio. — The neighbor always knows the neighborhood news.
Vi a mi vecina en el supermercado. — I saw my neighbor at the supermarket.
La vecina tiene un jardín hermoso. — The neighbor has a beautiful garden.
Invité a los vecinos a cenar el sábado. — I invited the neighbors to dinner on Saturday.
Mis vecinos me invitaron al bautizo de su bebé. — My neighbors invited me to their baby's baptism.
Todos los vecinos salieron a ver qué pasó. — All the neighbors came out to see what happened.

164 – tráfico | **traffic**

Esta ciudad tiene mucho tráfico. — This city has a lot of traffic.
A esta hora el tráfico es insoportable. — At this hour, traffic is unbearable.
Hay tráfico hasta en calles pequeñas. — There's traffic even on small streets.
Salí temprano para evitar el tráfico. — I left early to avoid traffic.
El tráfico es peor cuando llueve. — Traffic is worse when it rains.
Perdimos mucho tiempo en el tráfico. — We lost a lot of time in traffic.
El tráfico se detuvo por un accidente. — Traffic stopped because of an accident.
Estoy atorado en el tráfico. — I'm stuck in traffic.
El tráfico no avanza nada. — The traffic isn't moving at all.
El tráfico está fluido hoy, qué raro. — Traffic is smooth today, how strange.

165 – queso | **cheese**

¿Pones queso en tus tacos? — Do you put cheese on your tacos?
Pon el queso en el refrigerador. — Put the cheese in the refrigerator.
Ese queso huele fuerte, pero sabe muy bien. — That cheese smells strong, but it tastes really good.
El vino combina perfectamente con este queso. — The wine pairs perfectly with this cheese.
¿Es queso de vaca o de cabra? — Is it cow's cheese or goat's cheese?
Tienen muchos quesos interesantes en esa tienda. — They have lots of interesting cheeses at that store.
Compré dos quesos en el mercado. — I bought two cheeses at the market.
Me gustan los quesos suaves, no los fuertes. — I like mild cheeses, not strong ones.
Probamos tres quesos en la cata. — We tried three cheeses at the tasting.
Esos quesos combinan bien con vino tinto. — Those cheeses go well with red wine.

166 – dato	**fact, piece of information, data point**
Ese dato cambió mi opinión.	That fact changed my opinion.
Este dato confirma nuestra teoría.	This fact confirms our theory.
Necesito un dato más.	I need one more piece of information.
¿Tienes los datos completos?	Do you have all the data?
Los datos del estudio son claros.	The data from the study is clear.
Los datos no mienten.	The data doesn't lie.
Según los datos, todo va bien.	According to the data, everything's going well.
Los datos muestran un aumento del tres por ciento.	The data shows a 3% increase.
Tus datos valen mucho.	Your data is worth a lot.
Llena el formulario con tus datos.	Fill out the form with your information.

167 – sentimiento	**feeling**
No puedo explicar este sentimiento.	I can't explain this feeling.
Tengo un sentimiento raro desde ayer.	I've had a strange feeling since yesterday.
Hay un sentimiento de tristeza en el ambiente.	There's a feeling of sadness in the air.
El sentimiento de culpa no me deja dormir.	The feeling of guilt doesn't let me sleep.
Me cuesta trabajo expresar mis sentimientos.	I have a hard time expressing my feelings.
No puedo fingir mis sentimientos.	I can't fake my feelings.
Tengo sentimientos encontrados.	I have mixed feelings.
No lastimes los sentimientos de los demás.	Don't hurt other people's feelings.
Tengo sentimientos encontrados sobre eso.	I have mixed feelings about that.
No juegues con mis sentimientos.	Don't play with my feelings.

168 – paz	**peace**
Déjame en paz.	Leave me alone.
No me dejan en paz.	They won't leave me alone.
Descansa en paz, abuela querida.	Rest in peace, dear grandmother.
Me encanta la paz del campo.	I love the peace of the countryside.
Siento paz cuando camino por el bosque.	I feel peace when I walk through the woods.
Busco la paz interior a través de la meditación.	I seek inner peace through meditation.
El perdón trae paz al alma.	Forgiveness brings peace to the soul.
Los países firmaron un tratado de paz.	The countries signed a peace treaty.
La paz llegó después de años de conflicto.	Peace came after years of conflict.
Hicieron las paces con sus enemigos.	They made peace with their enemies.

169 – confianza | **trust, confidence**

Perdí la confianza en él. | I lost trust in him.
No quiero perder tu confianza. | I don't want to lose your trust.
Recuperar la confianza lleva tiempo. | Recovering trust takes time.
No tengo la confianza para decirle eso. | I don't have the confidence to tell him that.
Tengo plena confianza en tu capacidad. | I have complete confidence in your ability.
La confianza se gana con el tiempo. | Trust is earned over time.
Me lo dijo en confianza. | He told me in confidence.
Hay un ambiente de confianza aquí. | There's an atmosphere of trust here.
Sin confianza, nada funciona. | Without trust, nothing works.
Él apenas lo conoce y ya se toma confianzas. | He barely knows him and he's already acting familiar.

170 – negocio | **business**

Mi papá tiene un negocio de tortas. | My dad has a sandwich business.
Es un pequeño negocio familiar. | It's a small family business.
Él tiene cabeza para los negocios. | He has a head for business.
Mi hermana dirige el negocio en las tardes. | My sister runs the business in the afternoons.
Él está pensando en vender el negocio. | He's thinking about selling the business.
El negocio va bien este mes. | Business is going well this month.
El negocio no va tan bien. | The business isn't going so well.
Estoy pensando en poner un negocio propio. | I'm thinking of starting my own business.
Estos negocios locales viven del turismo. | These local businesses live off tourism.
Ella tiene varios negocios en el centro. | She has several shops downtown.

171 – tortilla | **tortilla (thin corn or wheat flatbread)**

Pásame una tortilla. | Pass me a tortilla.
Prefiero la tortilla de maíz que la de harina. | I prefer corn tortilla over flour tortilla.
Esta tortilla está recién hecha. | This tortilla is freshly made.
No hay nada como una tortilla hecha a mano. | There's nothing like a handmade tortilla.
La tortilla se usa en casi todas las comidas en México. | The tortilla is used in almost every meal in Mexico.
Siempre hay tortillas en la mesa de un mexicano. | There are always tortillas on a Mexican table.
Las tortillas van bien con todo. | Tortillas go well with everything.
Mi abuela hace tortillas a mano. | My grandmother makes tortillas by hand.
Las tortillas recién hechas huelen delicioso. | Freshly made tortillas smell delicious.
Echamos las tortillas en una canasta. | We put the tortillas in a basket.

172 – novio, novia | **boyfriend/fiancé/groom, girlfriend/fiancée/bride**

Mi novio y yo vamos al cine los viernes. | My boyfriend and I go to the movies on Fridays.
Mi novio compró los anillos de boda. | My fiancé bought the wedding rings.
El novio está esperando en el altar. | The groom is waiting at the altar.
Voy a recoger a mi novia a su trabajo. | I'm going to pick up my girlfriend from her work.
Mi novia y yo ya fijamos la fecha de la boda. | My fiancée and I already set the wedding date.
Puede besar a la novia. | You may kiss the bride.
¿Ya son novios? | Are they boyfriend and girlfriend now?
Mis novios siempre me engañaron. | My boyfriends always cheated on me.
Todas mis novias me han dejado. | All my girlfriends have left me.
Mis novias nunca me entendieron. | My girlfriends never understood me.

173 – frijol | **bean**

El frijol es un alimento esencial en México. | The bean is an essential food in Mexico.
¿Qué hay dentro de un frijol saltarín? | What is inside of a jumping bean?
Encontré un frijol negro entre los blancos. | I found a black bean among the white ones.
Los frijoles están listos. | The beans are ready.
Me encanta el arroz con frijoles. | I love rice with beans.
Arroz y frijoles nunca faltan en la mesa. | Rice and beans are never missing from the table.
Los frijoles son baratos y nutritivos. | Beans are cheap and nutritious.
Me gustan los frijoles con queso fresco. | I like beans with fresh cheese.
Mis hijos comen frijoles casi todos los días. | My kids eat beans almost every day.
Remoja los frijoles antes de cocinarlos. | Soak the beans before cooking them.

174 – foto | **picture, photo**

¿Puedo ver la foto que tomaste? | Can I see the photo you took?
Te mando una foto. | I'll send you a photo.
No me gusta cómo me veo en la foto. | I don't like how I look in the photo.
Borré la foto sin querer. | I deleted the photo by accident.
Subí una foto nueva a mi perfil. | I uploaded a new photo to my profile.
Esa foto fue tomada en la playa. | That photo was taken at the beach.
La foto quedó increíble. | The photo turned out amazing.
Perdí todas mis fotos del celular. | I lost all my photos from my phone.
Guardo todas mis fotos en la nube. | I save all my photos in the cloud.
Me encanta ver fotos antiguas de mis abuelos. | I love looking at old photos of my grandparents.

175 – clima	**weather, climate**
El clima hoy está perfecto.	The weather today is perfect.
Me gusta el clima de esta región.	I like the climate of this region.
El clima cambió de golpe.	The weather changed all of a sudden.
Odio cuando el clima no se decide.	I hate when the weather can't make up its mind.
Con este clima es mejor quedarse en casa.	With this weather it's better to stay home.
Ojalá el clima aguante para la fiesta.	Hopefully the weather holds up for the party.
El clima está cambiando rápidamente.	The climate is changing rapidly.
He vivido en climas muy distintos.	I have lived in very different climates.
Los climas fríos me gustan más.	I like cold climates better.
Me cuestan los climas muy húmedos.	Very humid climates are hard for me.

176 – ruido	**noise**
Ese ruido me asustó.	That noise scared me.
No puedo dormir con todo ese ruido.	I can't sleep with all that noise.
Cierra la ventana, entra mucho ruido.	Close the window, too much noise is coming in.
Los niños están haciendo demasiado ruido.	The kids are making too much noise.
Los vecinos hicieron mucho ruido anoche.	The neighbors made a lot of noise last night.
Me despertó un ruido raro.	A strange noise woke me up.
Deja de hacer ruido, estoy trabajando.	Stop making noise, I'm working.
Quiero vivir donde no haya tanto ruido.	I want to live where there isn't so much noise.
¿De dónde vienen esos ruidos?	Where are those noises coming from?
La licuadora está haciendo ruidos extraños.	The blender is making strange noises.

177 – culpa	**fault, blame, guilt**
No es mi culpa.	It's not my fault.
¿De quién fue la culpa?	Whose fault was it?
La culpa fue mía, lo siento mucho.	The fault was mine, I'm very sorry.
Ella siente culpa por lo que pasó.	She feels guilt for what happened.
Llegamos tarde por tu culpa.	We were late because of you.
Ustedes siempre me echan la culpa.	You guys always blame me.
La culpa me está matando.	The guilt is killing me.
Echar la culpa a alguien es fácil.	Putting the blame on someone is easy.
No busques culpas, busca soluciones.	Don't look for blame, look for solutions.
No cargues con las culpas de otros.	Don't carry the blame for others.

178 – jugo | **juice**

¿Quieres un jugo de naranja? | Do you want an orange juice?
Prefiero jugo de sandía, si tienes. | I prefer watermelon juice if you have it.
Voy a hacer jugo de sandía. | I'm going to make watermelon juice.
Derramé el jugo en la mesa. | I spilled the juice on the table.
Me gusta tomar jugo en el desayuno. | I like to drink juice at breakfast.
¿Has probado mezclar jugo con agua mineral? | Have you tried mixing juice with sparkling water?
¿Qué sabores de jugos tienes? | What juice flavors do you have?
En el colegio les dan jugos pequeños a los niños. | At school they give the kids small juices.
Los jugos recién hechos son mejores. | Freshly made juices are better.
Los jugos de frutas tropicales son deliciosos. | Tropical fruit juices are delicious.

179 – chile | **chili pepper**

¿Quieres chile? | Do you want chili pepper?
No le pongas chile. | Don't put chili pepper on it.
Este chile pica muchísimo. | This chili pepper is super spicy.
No aguanto el chile. | I can't handle chili pepper.
Le echaste mucho chile. | You put too much chili pepper in it.
Me gusta el chile, pero no tan picante. | I like chili pepper, but not too spicy.
Me gusta el chile relleno. | I like stuffed chili pepper.
No todos los chiles pican igual. | Not all chili peppers are equally spicy.
Necesito tres chiles para la receta. | I need three chili peppers for the recipe.
Compré chiles para hacer salsa. | I bought chili peppers to make salsa.

180 – esposo, esposa | **spouse, husband, wife**

Mi esposo es mi mejor amigo. | My husband is my best friend.
Te presento a mi esposo. | Let me introduce you to my husband.
Mi esposo cocina mejor que yo. | My husband cooks better than I do.
Su esposo la apoya en todo. | Her husband supports her in everything.
Él viaja con su esposa cada verano. | He travels with his wife every summer.
Mi esposa y yo estamos celebrando diez años de casados. | My wife and I are celebrating ten years of marriage.
Mi esposa merece lo mejor. | My wife deserves the best.
Mi esposa está embarazada. | My wife is pregnant.
Nuestros esposos se hicieron buenos amigos. | Our husbands became good friends.
Sus esposas se llevan muy bien. | Their wives get along very well.

181 – paseo — **walk, stroll, ride, outing**

Necesito un paseo para despejar la mente. — I need a stroll to clear my mind.
Me voy de paseo. — I'm going out for a walk.
Dimos un paseo por el centro. — We took a walk through downtown.
El paseo en bicicleta duró dos horas. — The bike ride lasted two hours.
El paseo en globo estuvo increíble. — The hot air balloon ride was incredible.
El paseo en barco fue muy divertido. — The boat ride was a lot of fun.
Los paseos por la playa siempre me relajan. — Walks on the beach always relax me.
Los paseos con mi familia son lo mejor. — Outings with my family are the best.
Me gustan mucho los paseos nocturnos. — I really like evening walks.
Los paseos en bicicleta me animan. — Bike rides cheer me up.

182 – ejercicio — **exercise**

Empecé una rutina de ejercicio nueva. — I started a new exercise routine.
El ejercicio es parte de mi vida diaria. — Exercise is part of my daily life.
El ejercicio me hace sentir bien. — Exercise makes me feel good.
¿Hiciste ejercicio hoy? — Did you exercise today?
No tuve tiempo de hacer ejercicio hoy. — I didn't have time to exercise today.
No me gusta hacer ejercicio. — I don't like to exercise.
Los ejercicios de matemáticas estaban difíciles. — The math exercises were hard.
Los ejercicios de este capítulo son más fáciles. — The exercises in this chapter are easier.
Hacemos ejercicios de estiramiento antes de correr. — We do stretching exercises before running.
Los ejercicios de respiración me ayudan a calmarme. — Breathing exercises help me calm down.

183 – cita — **appointment, date**

¿A qué hora es tu cita con el doctor? — What time is your appointment with the doctor?
Tengo una cita con el dentista a las cuatro. — I have an appointment with the dentist at four.
No quiero llegar tarde a la cita. — I don't want to be late to the appointment.
Él me invitó a una cita. — He asked me out on a date.
Tengo una cita esta noche. — I have a date tonight.
Es nuestra primera cita y estoy nervioso. — It's our first date and I'm nervous.
Nuestra primera cita fue en un café. — Our first date was at a café.
No he tenido una cita en meses. — I haven't had a date in months.
Después de varias citas, empezamos a salir en serio. — After several dates, we started dating seriously.
Hoy tengo dos citas médicas. — Today I have two medical appointments.

184 – muchacho, muchacha — **young man, young lady**

Ese muchacho ya maneja. — That young man already drives.
Oye, muchacho, ven acá. — Hey, young man, come here.
El muchacho ayuda en el rancho. — The boy helps on the ranch.
La muchacha cuida a los niños. — The girl takes care of the children.
Muchacha, ¿me puedes ayudar? — Young lady, can you help me?
La muchacha del café siempre es muy amigable. — The girl at the café is always very friendly.
Los muchachos entrenan en el gimnasio a las seis. — The guys train in the gym at six.
Los muchachos cargaron las mesas. — The young men carried the tables.
Las muchachas y yo fuimos al cine. — The girls and I went to the movies.
Las muchachas organizaron el evento. — The young women organized the event.

185 – pueblo — **town, people**

Mi abuelo nació en un pueblo pequeño. — My grandfather was born in a small town.
El pueblo está a dos horas de la ciudad. — The town is two hours from the city.
Todos se saludan en el pueblo. — Everyone greets each other in the town.
El pueblo tiene una sola gasolinera. — The town has only one gas station.
El pueblo entero salió a celebrar el festival. — The entire town came out to celebrate the festival.
El gobierno debe escuchar al pueblo. — The government should listen to the people.
En los pueblos pequeños no hay muchas opciones. — In small towns there aren't many options.
Los pueblos más alejados no tienen hospital. — The most remote towns don't have a hospital.
Muchos pueblos ya no tienen jóvenes. — Many towns no longer have young people.
Los pueblos indígenas preservan sus lenguas. — Indigenous peoples preserve their languages.

186 – cerveza — **beer**

¿Quieres una cerveza? — Do you want a beer?
Estoy tomando una cerveza. ¿Me acompañas? — I'm having a beer. Will you join me?
No quiero cerveza, gracias. — I don't want beer, thanks.
¿Hay cerveza sin alcohol? — Is there non-alcoholic beer?
Con este calor cae bien una cerveza fría. — In this heat, a cold beer hits the spot.
La cerveza mexicana es famosa en todo el mundo. — Mexican beer is famous around the world.
Compré cervezas para la fiesta. — I bought beers for the party.
¿Metiste las cervezas al refrigerador? — Did you put the beers in the refrigerator?
Las cervezas están en el refrigerador. — The beers are in the refrigerator.
Las cervezas ya están frías. — The beers are already cold.

187 – tío, tía | **uncle, aunt**

Mi tío siempre cuenta chistes. | My uncle always tells jokes.
¿Conoces a mi tío Roberto? | Do you know my uncle Roberto?
Mi tío es como un padre para mí. | My uncle is like a father to me.
Mi tía vive en Perú con su familia. | My aunt lives in Peru with her family.
Mi tía hace los mejores tamales. | My aunt makes the best tamales.
Mi mamá y mi tía son muy cercanas. | My mom and aunt are really close.
Mi tía me cuida cuando mis papás salen. | My aunt takes care of me when my parents go out.
Mis tíos me invitaron a la playa. | My uncles invited me to the beach.
Soy muy cercano con todos mis tíos y tías. | I'm close with all my aunts and uncles.
Mis tías preparan la comida para Navidad. | My aunts prepare the food for Christmas.

188 – principio | **start, beginning, principle**

Empecemos por el principio. | Let's start from the beginning.
Al principio me caía mal, pero ahora somos amigos. | At first I didn't like him, but now we're friends.
El principio de la historia me dejó confundido. | The beginning of the story left me confused.
El principio del libro es aburrido, pero sigue leyendo. | The beginning of the book is boring, but keep reading.
Desde el principio vimos que sería complicado. | From the start we saw it would be complicated.
Eso estaba claro desde el principio. | That was clear from the start.
Mi papá es un hombre de principios muy firmes. | My dad is a man of very firm principles.
No puedo traicionar mis principios solo por dinero. | I can't betray my principles just for money.
No todos compartimos los mismos principios. | Not all of us share the same principles.
Es una persona sin principios, capaz de cualquier cosa. | He's a person without principles, capable of anything.

189 – primo | **cousin**

Mi primo es como un hermano para mí. | My cousin is like a brother to me.
Mi primo y yo crecimos juntos. | My cousin and I grew up together.
Ese primo vive a dos cuadras de mi casa. | That cousin lives two blocks from my house.
Mi prima y yo tenemos los mismos abuelos. | My cousin and I have the same grandparents.
Soy muy cercana a mi prima. | I'm really close to my cousin.
Mi prima se casó el año pasado en Cancún. | My cousin got married last year in Cancún.
Todos mis primos viven por aquí. | All my cousins live around here.
¿Cuántos primos tienes en total? | How many cousins do you have in total?
No he visto a mis primos desde hace tiempo. | I haven't seen my cousins in a while.
Mis primos y yo jugamos mucho de niños. | My cousins and I played a lot as kids.

190 – señal	**signal, sign**
No hay señal de celular en esta zona.	There's no cell phone signal in this area.
No vi la señal de alto.	I didn't see the stop sign.
Ella no me dio ninguna señal de que él estaba molesto.	She didn't give me any sign that he was upset.
Una fiebre alta es una señal de que algo no anda bien.	A high fever is a sign that something's not right.
Dame una señal cuando estés listo para que salgamos.	Give me a signal when you're ready so we can leave.
Es buena señal que hayan contestado tan rápido.	It's a good sign that they answered so quickly.
El semáforo es una señal para detenerse.	The traffic light is a signal to stop.
¿Cuáles son las primeras señales del embarazo?	What are the first signs of pregnancy?
Pusieron señales de peligro cerca del acantilado.	They put up danger signs near the cliff.
Hay señales de precaución por toda la zona.	There are caution signs throughout the area.

191 – solución	**solution**
Encontramos una solución simple.	We found a simple solution.
Esa no es la mejor solución.	That's not the best solution.
Necesitamos una solución rápida.	We need a quick solution.
No hay solución fácil para este problema.	There isn't an easy solution to this problem.
Mi hermana siempre encuentra la solución a todo.	My sister always finds the solution to everything.
Esa es la solución más práctica que he escuchado.	That's the most practical solution I've heard.
Buscamos soluciones prácticas.	We're looking for practical solutions.
Analizamos varias posibles soluciones.	We analyzed several possible solutions.
Presentaron sus soluciones al equipo.	They presented their solutions to the team.
Encontraron distintas soluciones al mismo problema.	They found different solutions to the same problem.

192 – pierna	**leg**
¿Qué le pasó a su pierna?	What happened to his leg?
Él se rompió la pierna jugando fútbol.	He broke his leg playing soccer.
¿Cómo te hiciste esa cicatriz en tu pierna?	How did you get that scar on your leg?
Él tiene un tatuaje en la pierna derecha.	He has a tattoo on the right leg.
Estiro mis piernas cada mañana.	I stretch my legs every morning.
Me duelen las piernas después de correr tanto.	My legs hurts after running so much.
Mis piernas están adoloridas por el ejercicio de ayer.	My legs are sore from yesterday's workout.
Me tiemblan las piernas por el esfuerzo.	My legs are shaking from the effort.
Me pican las piernas por los mosquitos.	My legs itch because of the mosquitoes.
Ella se afeita las piernas cada semana.	She shaves her legs every week.

193 – campo | **countryside, field**

Crecí en el campo, no en la ciudad. | I grew up in the countryside, not in the city.
En el campo todo se siente más lento. | Everything feels slower in the countryside.
El silencio del campo me hace dormir mejor. | The silence of the countryside makes me sleep better.
Murieron muchos en el campo de batalla. | Many died on the battlefield.
La selección nacional está en el campo. | The national team is on the field.
El campo está en malas condiciones. | The field is in bad condition.
Sembramos los campos en marzo. | We plant the fields in March.
En esos campos pastan muchas vacas. | Many cows graze in those fields.
Los campos están cercados con alambre. | The fields are enclosed with wire.
Los campos deportivos están ocupados hoy. | The sports fields are busy today.

194 – edificio | **building**

Vivo en este edificio. | I live in this building.
El edificio tiene diez pisos. | The building has ten floors.
El edificio tiene piscina en la azotea. | The building has a pool on the rooftop.
Hay un restaurante en la planta baja del edificio. | There's a restaurant on the ground floor of the building.
Ese es el edificio más alto del país. | That is the tallest building in the country.
Los edificios modernos usan mucho vidrio. | Modern buildings use a lot of glass.
Los edificios viejos tienen más encanto. | Old buildings have more charm.
Esos edificios se ven abandonados. | Those buildings look abandoned.
Convirtieron los edificios en museos. | They converted the buildings into museums.
Los edificios están conectados por túneles. | The buildings are connected by tunnels.

195 – esquina | **corner**

Dobla en la siguiente esquina. | Turn at the next corner.
Vivo en la esquina. | I live on the corner.
Mi casa es la de la esquina. | My house is the one on the corner.
Te espero en la esquina. | I'll wait for you at the corner.
Hay un puesto de tacos en la esquina. | There's a taco stand on the corner.
Cruza en la esquina, no por la mitad de la calle. | Cross at the corner, not in the middle of the street.
Hay una panadería a la vuelta de la esquina. | There's a bakery just around the corner.
Me pegué con la esquina de la mesa. | I hit myself on the corner of the table.
Las hojas están dobladas en las esquinas. | The pages are bent at the corners.
Las esquinas del parque tienen bancas. | The park's corners have benches.

196 – sonido

sound

El sonido de tu voz me calma.
The sound of your voice calms me.

Me gusta el sonido de la lluvia.
I like the sound of rain.

El sonido de los truenos me asusta.
The sound of thunder scares me.

No hay sonido más bonito que la risa de un niño.
There's no sound more beautiful than a child's laughter.

El sonido viaja más rápido en el agua.
Sound travels faster in water.

El sonido del mar me relaja.
The sound of the sea relaxes me.

Se pueden escuchar los sonidos del mar desde aquí.
One can hear the sounds of the sea from here.

Me encantan los sonidos de las olas al romper.
I love the sounds of the waves breaking.

Los perros pueden oír sonidos que los humanos no.
Dogs can hear sounds that humans can't.

Hay sonidos que solo los perros pueden escuchar.
There are sounds that only dogs can hear.

197 – bebida

drink, beverage

¿Te apetece alguna bebida antes de cenar?
Would you like a drink before dinner?

Tráeme una bebida, por favor.
Bring me a drink, please.

Necesito una bebida refrescante.
I need a refreshing drink.

Mi bebida favorita es la horchata.
My favorite drink is horchata.

La bebida es gratis con la comida.
The drink is free with the meal.

¿Cuánto cuestan las bebidas aquí?
How much do the drinks cost here?

Las bebidas son caras aquí.
The drinks are expensive here.

Compré bebidas para la fiesta.
I bought drinks for the party.

Las bebidas están en el refrigerador.
The drinks are in the refrigerator.

No tomo bebidas con cafeína por la noche.
I don't drink caffeinated beverages at night.

198 – flor

flower

¿Quién te regaló esa flor tan bonita?
Who gave you that pretty flower?

Pon la flor en un florero.
Put the flower in a vase.

¿Qué tipo de flor es esa?
What type of flower is that?

Mi flor favorita es el girasol.
My favorite flower is the sunflower.

Las flores atraen mariposas y abejas.
Flowers attract butterflies and bees.

Las flores huelen muy bien.
The flowers smell so good.

Venden flores en la esquina.
They sell flowers on the corner.

Mi abuela tiene todo tipo de flores en su jardín.
My grandma has all kinds of flowers in her garden.

Corté unas flores para decorar.
I cut some flowers to decorate.

A mi esposa no le gusta que le regalen flores.
My wife doesn't like being given flowers.

199 – techo | **roof, ceiling**

El techo gotea cada vez que llueve. | The roof leaks every time it rains.
El techo de mi casa necesita reparación. | The roof of my house needs repair.
Necesitamos un techo nuevo. | We need a new roof.
El techo se cambió hace solo dos años. | The roof was replaced only two years ago.
El gato se subió al techo otra vez. | The cat climbed onto the roof again.
El techo de la iglesia es altísimo. | The church ceiling is very high.
Hay una gotera en el techo del baño. | There's a leak in the bathroom ceiling.
Los techos de tejas son muy comunes aquí. | Tile roofs are very common here.
Muchos techos en esta ciudad son azules. | Many roofs in this town are blue.
Los techos altos mantienen la casa fresca. | High ceilings keep the house cool.

200 – mente | **mind**

Mantén la mente abierta. | Keep an open mind.
Ella tiene una mente brillante. | She has a brilliant mind.
Su mente está llena de ideas creativas. | Her mind is full of creative ideas.
Me vino a la mente tu nombre. | Your name came to my mind.
Mi mente divaga cuando estoy cansado. | My mind wanders when I'm tired.
No puedo sacarlo de mi mente. | I can't get it out of my mind.
Tengo muchas cosas en la mente. | I have many things on my mind.
Las mentes creativas cambian el mundo. | Creative minds change the world.
Necesitamos a las mentes más brillantes del país. | We need the brightest minds in the country.
Las mentes jóvenes aprenden rápido. | Young minds learn quickly.

www.ingramcontent.com/pod-product-compliance
Lightning Source LLC
LaVergne TN
LVHW080315110826
845155LV00023B/127

* 9 7 8 1 9 5 2 1 6 1 1 5 5 *